CANADIAN FORCES

AN HISTORICAL SALUTE TO THOSE ON THE FRONT LINE

Art Montague

Published by
MacIntyre Purcell Publishing Inc.
232 Lincoln St., PO Box 1142
Lunenburg, Nova Scotia
B0J 2C0 Canada
www.macintyrepurcell.com

We acknowledge the support of the Department of Canadian Heritage and the Nova Scotia Department of Communities, Culture and Heritage in the development of writing and publishing in Canada.

Printed and bound in Canada by Marquis Imprimeur Inc.

Cover photo by Adrien Veczan.

Library and Archives Canada Cataloguing in Publication
Montague, Art
Canadian Forces : an historical salute to those
on the front line / Art Montague.

ISBN 978-1-926916-09-5

1. Canada--History, Military. 2. Canada--Armed
Forces--History. 3. Canada. Canadian Armed
Forces--History. I. Title.

UA600.M64 2011   355.00971   C2011-903956-7

ACKNOWLEDGMENTS

Just as no man is an island, no book is solely the writer's. This book is a case in point.

Foremost, I think of the historians, journalists, and memoirists who have meticulously documented the activities of the men and women of Canada's military over these many years. They have provided the foundation—the bricks and mortar—for this book.

The professional team at MacIntyre-Purcell Publishing has done a remarkable job. I cannot say enough about the unswerving confidence publisher John MacIntyre demonstrated from conception of this project to the book now in hand.

Lynn McCarron was more than the editor of this book. From the beginning she had a vision and went about crafting the material she was given to reflect that vision. She made the book her own while keeping it mine—a rare editorial achievement.

Katelyn Matheson also had a vision. When, in her painstaking research, she saw a picture that best reflected the heart of each story, she knew it and made every attempt required to get it. Kudos go out to her for her resourcefulness and determination.

For the images, a heartfelt thank you goes out to all our generous contributors, public and private. A special mention should be made to Library and Archives Canada, Legion Magazine, The National War Museum, The War Amps and the Canadian Forces Joint Imagery Centre.

Finally, the best for last, my wife, Joanne. She is the person who kept this project moving forward even as I sometimes despaired that it would never be completed. She has always been the first editor of my books, this one included. I write in longhand and she has the onerous task of deciphering my scrawl and transcribing it to the computer. It's a task I wouldn't wish on anyone.

Over the course of researching and writing this book I have developed an enormous respect for the men and women of the Canadian Forces, past and present. I hope this respect is adequately conveyed in the book for, indeed, this is one of the book's intents.

Art Montague

CONTENTS

Timeline...Richard Pierpoint: A Life to Remember...As Good As It Gets: The
Victoria Cross...Torching T.O....Remember the Engineers...The Canadian:
Our Horse, Of Course....With Respect to Military Nursing....Victoria Cross
Vignettes: Alexander Dunn: The First V.C. Recipient...William C. Hall: A
Canadian Soldier in the British Navy...Cockburn, Turner and Holland: Legends
of Leliefontein...Timothy O'Hea: The One and Only...Frederick Fisher: The
Hero From St. Catherines...Sam Steele: The First Peacekeeper...Snipers, The
Vanguard of Special Forces.

World War I....Remembering John McCrea...In Flanders Fields....Arthur Currie:
Canada's Citizen General...McBride's Navy: An Executive Decision...No White
Man's War: 2nd Construction Battalion...Passchendaele –Hell For Any Soldier...
Billie Barker: The Love of Flying....1st Newfoundland at Somme: A Generation
on the Line...Sergeant Thomas Ricketts, VC: A Teen-Age Hero...Orpington,
An Atypical Olde English Town...Halifax Explosion...The Homefront: Good
Times, Bad Times, And The Tax Man...Frederick Fisher: The Hero From St.
Catherines...Bishop and Beurling: The Killer Bs...Vimy Memorial: Vision of A
Victory...Winnie the Pooh: The Story of A Mascot...Siberian Sojourn.

World War Ill...Prelude To Peril...The Pal From Gander...Sergeant-Major John
Osborn: To The Last...Canada's Shame: The Hong Kong Story...Reverend John
Weir Foote: Duty Bound...Name These Tunes PAGE 4-5...The Cheap And

Nasties…Halifax: The Convoy City…Halifax: The Mob Rules…HMCS Athabasca: Canada's Hard Luck Ship…The Princes Go To War…Iceburg Ahoy…Sino-Canadian Soldiering…Loyalty Rewarded…The Invasion Of North America… Private Ernest "Smoky" Smith: Big Man In A Small Bottle…The Song of the D-Day Dodgers…The Canadians Face Off…The Ortona Toast…Prince Of Warriors…To Have And Have Not: Antwerp…Tommy Burns: In War And Peace.

FOREWORD

BY SCOTT TAYLOR

In his book, *Canadian Forces: An Historical Salute To Those On The Front Line,* author Art Montague successfully accomplishes his goal of paying tribute to the Canadian defence community.

While traditional military histories chronicle the events of certain battles, the exploits of select individuals or the collective accomplishment of a particular military unit, *An Historical Salute* encompasses all the achievements, by all service branches, including Reserves and Cadets, then and now.

Montague understands well that the Canadian Forces are not a stand-alone entity and that once a soldier becomes a veteran he does not cease his affiliation with the warrior caste.

The very scope of this book means that the tales are told in bite-size samplers, but this only adds to the effectiveness of Montague's portrayal of Canada's military as an exciting, colourful institution.

This book would make an ideal teaching aid for history teachers to liven up their lessons with interesting anecdotes and factoids. For those within the defence community, it provides not only a positive reflection on their own trade and history, but also an interesting peek at the other branches with whom they serve.

Montague includes short biographies on some of Canada's famous military leaders such as General Arthur Currie and Commander Eedson (Tommy) Burns, as well as profiles of virtually unknown soldiers from the ranks.

From the monumental, such as major historical battles, to the mundane—like domestic aid-to-civil-power, right down to the minutiae, including the contents of ration packs, Montague provides a top to bottom book of all things Canadian Military.

What is very refreshing is that the writing style captures the same lighthearted wit that embodies the spirit of our service members.

Tribute is also paid to organizations such as The War Amps and the Royal Canadian Legion, who ensure that veterans not only receive financial benefits, but also the respect and admiration of the Canadian public.

From a personal perspective it was touching to see war correspondents receive a bravo-zulu from the author, and especially so since my colleagues and I received a mention.

This book is truly a salute to all those in uniform, and I wish to wholeheartedly return that salute to the author.

Scott Taylor is a Canadian writer and journalist who specializes in military and war reporting. His coverage has included wars in Cambodia, Africa, the Balkans and most recently, Iraq. Taylor is a former private in the Canadian Forces, and is now the editor and publisher of *Esprit de Corps*, a military magazine.

Taylor's published works include *Unembedded: Two Decades of Maverick War Reporting*, *INAT: Images of Serbia and the Kosovo Conflict* and *Tarnished Brass: Crime and Corruption in the Canadian Military*.

INTRODUCTION

This book was not written to serve as a comprehensive history of the Canadian military from it's inception. There is much more to the Canadian Forces than our soldiers' statistical contributions in the world wars and other combat zones and much more than its international peacekeeping and disaster relief.

To look at Canada's military history from a statistical or chronological standpoint does, in this author's opinion, a disservice to the spirit of Canada, and to our inborn appreciation for a great story.

Canada's military history has tales to tell as diverse as its people, as diverse as its enormous physical expanse. The unique and surprising endeavors attempted and achieved by our forces deserve a closer look than history has generally granted.

This book celebrates heroes like General Arthur Curry, who revolutionized the treatment and stature of Canadians at war, refusing to fit into the role assumed for them under British command; two of the most celebrated WWI flying Aces, Bishop and Barker, who came literally out of the blue, from a country with no air force; Joel McCrea, who wrote the definitive poem expressing the tragic reality of war while sitting next to Flanders' Fields in 1915, a poem that resonates as strongly today as it ever did.

And the Royal Newfoundland Regiment at the Battle of Beaumont-Hamel, an entire generation of young men sacrificed in a clearly hopeless endeavour.

This book tells the story of giant aircraft carriers made of ice, a WWII proposal spearheaded by Winston Churchill, and Operation Muskox, the plan to determine that Canada's North could never sustain a presence of ground forces; the Canadian ground forces in the Italian Campaign, possibly the most feared fighters in WWII; fiercest of warriors, Tommy Prince, one of the creators of the much-feared Devil's Brigade; and "Sergeant" Gander, a Newfoundland dog that grabbed a grenade in his teeth and ran away with it, saving the lives of his company.

A salute goes out to the active Canadian Forces, plus the Reserves and Cadets, who are regularly called on to assist with disaster relief -- floods, forest fires, ice and snow storms, and to the Forces' maritime search and rescue missions along thousands of kilometres of coastline, whatever the weather.

The relevance of the Canadian Forces is also celebrated in acknowledging the community efforts of thousands of veterans through their involvements in such organizations as the Royal Canadian Legion and War Amps.

This book tells the intimate and personal stories of just a few of the amazing characters from our country's military past. These are tales of of valour, integrity and the huge presence of Canadian soldiers.

"He will win who knows when to fight and when not to fight. He will win who knows how to handle both superior and inferior forces. He will win who army is animated by the same spirit throughout all its ranks. He will win who, prepared himself, waits to take the enemy unprepared. He will win who has military capacity and is not interfered with by the sovereign."

— Sun Tzu

CHAPTER I:
NATION BUILDING

Military campaigns and treaties between France and Britain began defining geographic boundaries and the temper of "northern colonies and colonists" long before Canada became a nation.

After Britain lost her southern colonies in the American Revolution, the U.S. became her enemy, and by extension, an enemy of Upper and Lower Canada as well. Affection and loyalty for Britain was much stronger in Upper Canada, where the population included many Loyalists fleeing the revolution, versus the largely Quebecois population of Lower Canada.

When the U.S. invaded Canada to attack British forces in the War of 1812, the British were able to recruit militia in both Canadas to fight back: Lower Canadians, who were not interested in a watered-down version of British rule, and Upper Canadians, who were already inclined to be anti-American and pro-British.

The conflict was settled by European powers, and the settlers who had fought against the Americans knew that their "country" had been considered little more than a backwater battlefield. It was not a backwater to them, however, and the seeds of national sentiment had been sown. Settlers began to envision the birth of an independent country, perhaps even two.

While Canada was under British rule, professional soldiering was primarily a British responsibility. Even after Confederation, British traditions and training continued to have a strong influence. Developing a wholly Canadian officer corps was a long and slow process.

Although the British felt obliged to request permission of the Canadian government to recruit for the Crimean War and then again for the Boer War, they still controlled Canada's defence and foreign policy, a situation that did not formally change until the 1930s.

The British did gradually pull out of active garrisoning in Canada. Although Canada would retain a military reliance on the British, it had built the nucleus of the trained professional officers and experienced troops essential for defence.

W. H. Bartlett. Locks on the Rideau Canal (detail), 1841, engraving print, Bytown Museum
Photo: Graham Iddon, Bytown Museum, P1408

11

TIMELINE

First Nations people, of course, were involved in sophisticated military campaigns long before Europeans arrived. Military activity involving Europeans began in Canada's geographic domain as far back as the 16th and 17th centuries when European nations jockeyed with each other for control, and indigenous peoples struggled to maintain their very existence. Nevertheless, the War of 1812 provided the first hint of a nation in the making. And from then. . .

1835 CRIMEAN WAR – British allowed to recruit, 5,000 militia answer call

MAY 31, 1866 – Fenians near Fort Erie, Battle of Ridgeway

1871 – Military training schools set up at Kingston and Quebec City, first full-time professionals Canadian soldiers

1876 – Prime Minister Alexander Mackenzie sets up Royal Military College

DEC. 1876 – Queen's Own Rifles called on to disperse Grand Trunk Railway strikers

1884 – British allowed to recruit 400 "voyageurs" for Nile expedition to relieve Khartoum in Sudan

1885 – Maj.-Gen. Frederick Middleton, GOC Canadian Militia defeats Métis at Batoche (May 11)

1898 – Protecting sovereignty during Klondike Gold Rush, Yukon Field Force of 200 volunteers dispatched, half of whom stay in Dawson Creek until June 2, 1900

OCTOBER 30, 1899 – 1,000 volunteers in Royal Canadian Regiment depart for Capetown (Transvaal)

FEBRUARY 18-27, 1900 – Canadian victory at Paardeberg Drift despite 40-degree temperature and rain, plus poor equipment

NOVEMBER 1900 – Three Royal Canadian Dragoons win Victoria Crosses in same action

JUNE 1902 – Boer War ends

MAY 4, 1910 – Official formation of Royal Canadian Navy

AUGUST 4, 1914 – Great Britain declares war on Germany and Austria-Hungary

OCTOBER 14, 1914 – First Canadian troops arrive in England

APRIL 22, 1915 – 2nd Battle of Ypres, Canadian troops subjected to poison gas

FEBRUARY-DECEMBER 1916 – Battle of Verdun, one million casualties overall

JULY-NOVEMBER 1916 – Battle of Somme

APRIL-MAY 1917 – Battle of Arras

APRIL 19, 1917 – Battle of Vimy Ridge, Canadians distinguish themselves

OCTOBER 28, 1917 – Battle of Passchendaele, Canadian victory

Signore Tomasso, an Italian barber, cuts the hair of Private R.J. Tims of the Anti-Aircraft Support Company, Saskatoon Light Infantry (M.G.). Watched by Private Tommy Bear, Ortona, Italy, 10 January 1944.

TIMELINE

JANUARY 1, 1918 – Conscription begins in Canada

APRIL 14, 1918 – Second Battle of Arras. Canadian and British troops prevail

AUGUST 1918 – Amiens assault commences

1924 – Royal Canadian Air Force officially formed

JULY 17, 1936 – Spanish Civil War begins, Canadians join International Brigade, and form the Mackenzie-Papineau Battalion

SEPTEMBER 10, 1939 – 10 days after Britain, Canada declares war on Germany

DECEMBER 15, 1939 – Canada agrees to train Allied pilots

OCTOBER 30, 1941 – Doomed Canadian force sails for Hong Kong

DECEMBER 25, 1941 – Canadians surrender at Hong Kong

APRIL 27, 1942 – Canadians vote for conscription

AUGUST 19, 1942 – Disastrous Dieppe raid

JULY 10, 1943 – Canadian troops involved in Sicily landings

DECEMBER 28, 1943 – Canadian victory at Ortona

JUNE 26, 1945 – United Nations Charter signed by 50 nations

1947-48 – First United Nations Commission in Korea

APRIL 4, 1948 – Canada joins in forming North American Treaty Organization

1949-1979 – Canadians act as UN military observers in India-Pakistan

JUNE 25, 1950 – Korean War begins, termed a police action

JULY 7, 1950 – Canada commits three destroyers and RCAF 426 Combat Squadron to Korean campaign

DEC.18, 1950 – First contingent of Canadian infantry troops arrives in Korea

MCPL. Cooney and Padre Melanson from Kingston on U.N. duty with the Canadian contingent in Rwanda.

JUNE 28, 1951 – First Commonwealth Division formed, comprising troops from Canada, Australia, New Zealand, India, United States

JULY 27, 1953 – Korean ceasefire signed, UN maintains presence to present day

1954 – UN presence in Middle East conflict including Israel/Egypt/Jordan/Lebanon/Syria

1954-1974 – UN presence in Cambodia-Laos-Vietnam

1956-57 – UN Emergency Force in Egypt

1958 – UN back in Lebanon

MAY 12, 1958 – Canada & U.S. sign NORAD joint defence agreement

1960-64 – UN active in Congo

1962-63 – UN active in West New Guinea

1963-64 – UN active in Yemen

MARCH 15, 1964 – UN active in Cyprus, still there

1965-66 – UN active in Dominican Republic

1965-66 – UN returns to Indian/Pakistan

TIMELINE

FEBRUARY 18, 1968 – Canadian Army/Navy/Air Force unified as Canadian Forces

1968-69 – UN active in Nigeria

OCTOBER 15, 1970 – FLQ crisis, Canadian troops enter Quebec City

OCTOBER 16, 1970 – War Measures Act invoked

JULY 31, 1973 – Canadian contingent of UN departs Vietnam

1973-79 – UN active again in Egypt

1974 – UN monitors Golan Heights

1978 – UN active in southern Lebanon

1979-80 – Commonwealth Monitoring Force, Rhodesia

1986 ONWARD – UN active in Sinai

1988-91 – UN observers in Iran-Iraq

1989 – UN active in Angola

1989-90 – UN active in Namibia, also in Central America

JULY 11, 1990 – Canadian Forces called in to Oka (Quebec) crisis

1990 – UN active in Afghanistan & Pakistan

1990-91 – Organization of American States active in Haiti

1990-91 – Gulf War begins, Canadian Forces contingent numbers 4,000+

1991 – UN active in Iraq-Kuwait; 1st Engineers Regiment from CFB Chilliwack active in mine clearing

1991 – UN active in Western Sahara, including Morocco

1991 – UN active in Angola

1991-92 – UN active in Cambodia

1991 – European Community and Canada active in Yugoslavia

1992 – UN active in El Salvador

1992 – UN active in Yugoslavia/Bosnia/Herzegovina/Serbia/Macedonia

1992 – UN active in Somalia

1993 – UN active in Mozambique

1994 – UN active in Dominican Republic

1994 – UN active in Uganda and Rwanda

1999 – NATO attacks Yugoslavia

2002 – War on Terror; Canadians to Middle East and Afghanistan

2011 – Canadian troops drawn down in Afghanistan

NOTE: Every U.N. mission listed has involved Canadian Forces.

Private Eric Hennie, a member of the Provincial Reconstruction Team Patrol Company at Camp Nathan Smith, Afghanistan.

RICHARD PIERPOINT: A LIFE TO REMEMBER

Soldiers fought and died for the cause of Canada's independence when the country was still a British colony. While these soldiers may have helped to shape the nation, many of their stories have fallen through the cracks of history. Richard Pierpoint's story is one that should never be forgotten.

A slave from Senegal, Pierpoint won his freedom by fighting for the Loyalists during the American Revolution. He fought with Butler's Rangers, considered the most successful British regiment in the north sector. After the war, Pierpoint, (along with many of the other Rangers), settled in the Niagara region on land grants provided by the British to United Empire Loyalists.

Although nearing 60 when the War of 1812 began, Pierpoint so valued his freedom in Upper Canada that he offered to form a "Corp of Men of Colour" to help fight for it. Although Britain had abolished slavery, prejudice still existed, and though the British acted on the Pierpoint's proposal, they formed their own Coloured Corps, commanded, of course, by a white officer. Pierpoint enlisted immediately. During the war, the corps saw action at the Battle of Queenston Heights, Fort George, and Lundy's Lane.

After the War of 1812, Pierpoint continued to pursue independence for blacks within Upper Canada. He was active in establishing black settlements, mostly small enclaves scattered over the Niagara frontier. In 1821, he founded the Garafraxas Settlement near present-day Fergus, Ont., a settlement that eventually became a terminal on the Underground Railway.

Although Richard Pierpoint would die in 1838 at 94 years old, he lived to see his fellow black colonists come together once again as a citizen militia, this time to help quell the Rebellion of 1837 in Upper Canada.

When the rebel William Lyon Mackenzie was forced to flee York (now Toronto), he holed up with about 600 men on Navy Island (American territory in the Niagara River above the Falls). Here, his force was regularly supplied by the American steamer *Caroline*. On the Canadian side of the river was a company of black volunteer militia, which had been hurriedly raised from Pierpoint's settlements.

On December 29, Upper Canada's government issued the order to capture the

Caroline. A small raiding party set off across the river and engaged the *Caroline's* crew, taking the ship. The *Caroline* was promptly set afire, then allowed to drift with the current, which sent it plummeting over what is now the most famous waterfall in all of North America.

TORCHING T.O.

Losing its American colonies in 1776 weighed heavily on the British, who viewed the loss as a crushing blow to their empire.

It came as little surprise that by 1812, they were back at war with the Americans, who had dared to side with the French in their seemingly endless disputes with the Brits. Pre-Confederation Canada was, in turn, forced to shoulder a share of this conflict.

On April 28, 1813, American Gen. Henry Dearborn sailed up the north shore of Lake Ontario and attacked York (now Toronto). York was defended by British regular soldiers and an on-call, 241-member militia, a motley crew of farmers and townspeople. The militia was obliged by law to answer the call to arms, even though the members were untrained and unpaid settlers, expected to provide their own arms, ammunition, uniforms and provisions in the name of the Crown.

LINCOLN MILITIA

At the close of the American Revolution, more than 800 members of Butler's Rangers became United Empire Loyalists, and many continued their militia activities. During the War of 1812, those living in the Niagara region (and, by this time, it now included their sons) served with distinction as the Lincoln Militia.

The Lincoln Militia evolved into the present-day Lincoln and Welland Regiment, a reserve infantry battalion and part of the 31st Canadian Brigade Group based in St. Catharines and Welland.

Members of the Lincs have seen active service in every UN peacekeeping mission and police action since the end of the Second World War. This also includes NATO actions, such as those in Afghanistan.

By the time the call to arms spread though the settlement and neighbouring countryside, the battle was over. A substantial contingent of British reinforcements had set up to do battle, but the troops were waiting for the Americans at the wrong place. Then, British soldiers in the main fort accidentally blew up the powder magazine, causing most of the battle's casualties. Within a few hours, Dearborn had won the day.

The famous Burning of York was not at all what it seemed. Townspeople pointed out government buildings to the invaders and helped with looting and burning them. Shops and houses remained intact, although some local merchants did submit substantial claims to the British for "losses" resulting from the invasion.

Throughout their time of glory, Dearborn's officers were kept busy "paroling" militia members. This was a common arrangement in those days because tending to prisoners of war was both costly and time-consuming. Parole was granted if the parolee swore not to take up arms again. By the end of the day, 1,400 settlers had received paroles, remarkable considering militia members on the British books numbered only 241.

The reason for the discrepancy was pretty straightforward: it was seeding time, and settlers wanted to get their spring planting done without delay. Many settlers did not take their militia duty seriously. Their annual summer "training exercises" usually involved a weekend parade, a picnic and substantial quantities of beer.

Dearborn sailed off victorious (he didn't even stay overnight). A few months later, however, he had to return to defend America's reputation. Since the Americans had left, some York locals had taken to looting their neighbours' houses and rustling their livestock in the name of the United States. As Dearborn arrived in the harbour, the local villains disappeared into the countryside. None were captured, but the thieving stopped.

It is unlikely the militia could have turned back the Americans at York. The militias of Upper and Lower Canada did, however, prove to be a decisive force in other engagements during the war. These included victories at Queenston Heights, Crysler's Farm, Chateauguay and Lundy's Lane.

While militia participation may have somewhat affirmed the country's loyalty to Britain, it also began to define the sense among the population that a new country and a national identity could be emerging, one unlike that of either the United States or Britain.

REMEMBERING THE ENGINEERS

The foundations of many Canadian cities were laid down in pre-Confederation times by military engineers to satisfy military defensive considerations. Only later did it occur to politicians and historians that what these engineers were really building was a nation.

French engineers built fortresses and harbours at Halifax and Quebec City. Britain's Royal Engineers would later improve upon both.

Recognizing the need to speed military supplies to Great Lakes settlements and garrisons, the Royal Engineers constructed canals on the St. Lawrence River and fortified the city of Kingston. Their work was the forerunner to the eventual St. Lawrence Seaway.

W. H. Bartlett. *The Rideau Canal, Bytown* (detail), 1841, engraving print, Bytown Museum, P1410.

Still considered an engineering marvel, the Rideau Canal connects Kingston to Ottawa. Part of an alternate route from Montreal to the Great Lakes, the canal was considered critical in the early 19th century in case American forces blockaded the St. Lawrence River.

Col. John By, the Royal Engineer who designed and oversaw the project, created, by extension, the city of Ottawa. at the northern head of the canal. His engineers surveyed and supervised the layout of the settlement. The Engineers also built many of Ottawa's first public buildings and houses. Between Ottawa, then named Bytown, and Hull, now Gatineau, By's engineers built the first bridge linking French and English Canada.

On the West Coast, the work of the Royal Engineers was no less important and no less enduring. Summoned to British Columbia to control an influx of thousands of Americans to the Cariboo Gold Rush — a potential threat to sovereignty in the area— the Engineers' military presence quickly and emphatically ensured law and order.

The Royal Engineers also surveyed town sites in the Lower Mainland, including New Westminster, and began the work that established Vancouver as the great port city it is today. Their work included construction of the Kingsway, for decades the main road connecting New Westminster to Vancouver.

An engineering feat to rival them all in the development of Canada is the Cariboo Road, the route to the gold fields. Its most difficult stretch was carved from the sheer cliffs of the Fraser River Canyon. This work of the Engineers was valued long after the gold strike petered out. The same route first surveyed by the Engineers was used when the transcontinental railroad was constructed. Later, it became the route of the Trans-Canada Highway.

The Royal Engineers were highly regarded in Canada. One of their number became the first commandant of Canada's Royal Military College. And they did not simply carry out their military duties and return to Britain. When their service ended, many stayed on with their families, continuing to contribute as private citizens to the stability and growth of the country.

THE CANADIAN: OUR HORSE, OF COURSE

From the Seven Years War in the 18th Century until the end of the First World War, Canada's national horse was involved in every domestic and overseas military campaign in which the country has taken part. Appropriately, the distinctive breed is named the *Canadian*. For good reasons, all of them Canadian, it also has another name: Little Iron Horse.

The *Canadian* had royal beginnings in the stables of Louis XIV at Versailles. Here

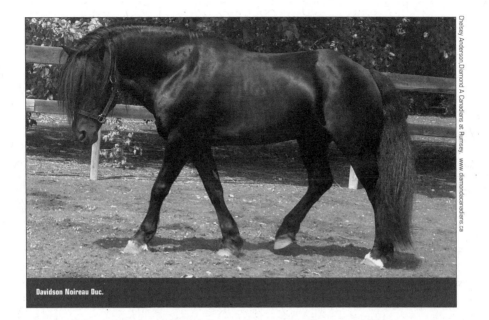

Davidson Noireau Duc.

Louis kept 600 of the finest stallions and mares he could gather from across Europe. Between 1665 and 1671, he sent 81 of his choicest animals to New France for the use of his officers and noblemen and to have them bred for labour.

The contrast between the Palace of Versailles and Canada's hinterland could not have been more stark. Many *Canadians* went instantly from royal comforts and pampering in France to a harsh, hardscrabble existence helping to clear land and log the forests. Still, their new life may have seemed a relief after a long voyage under sail across the Atlantic.

As to breeding, they did so in abundance. By the end of the 18th century, there were 150,000 *Canadians*. They were literally the only horses in New France.

Tough and Temperate

The horses descended from the king's finest adapted beautifully. Their endurance and strength were unsurpassed even by heavy horses like Belgians and Percherons. Teamed together, the *Canadians* exhausted the big fellas and twitched their ears and tails looking for more to do. They were also intelligent and gentle.

If oats and hay were in short supply, as they usually were, the *Canadians* foraged for themselves in the bush and swamps; poplar bark is still one of their favourite foods. And they could run; they made a name for themselves in carriage and sleigh races and also proved to be excellent trotters and pacers. Well-off colonists sometimes kept a "fancy" in their barns just for racing.

Into Battle

On the record, *Canadians* encountered their first military action during the Seven Years War, albeit on the losing side. Gen. Louis-Joseph de Montcalm is said to have ridden a *Canadian* stallion into the Battle of the Plains of Abraham. The *Canadians'* next foray wasn't much more successful; the British Army purchased 1,500 *Canadians* for service during the American Revolution.

The sale of *Canadians* to New Englanders helped spread the breed's reputation. Export sales skyrocketed. Some 30,000 were sold to the Union and Confederate armies during the U.S. Civil War. Unrecorded numbers were sent to the West Indies to work on sugar plantations. The Pony Express likely used some *Canadians*, and many U.S. stagecoach lines regularly harnessed them up. Some historians have suggested a few *Canadians* were at the Battle of Little Big Horn.

During the 19th century in Canada, *Canadians* hauled heavy arms, supplies and troops sent to quell the Northwest Rebellion. Later, they became the early horses of choice for the North West Mounted Police. In 1898, they carried troops to the Yukon to establish garrisons during the Klondike Gold Rush. Then came the Boer War and the First World War. Of the *Canadians* shipped to these last two wars, none came back. The number of purebreds continued to diminish. By the 1970s, fewer than 400 remained.

Alarmed, private breeders, mostly in Quebec and eastern Ontario, took matters into their own hands. Today, the breed is being carefully re-established. The breeders association now estimates the number of *Canadians* to be near 6,000. Nevertheless, they are still considered to be "rare," taking into account some three million other standard-bred horses are registered worldwide.

Rising Stars

In 1999, Quebec named the *Canadian* the province's official heritage horse. And in 2002, with an Act of Parliament, the federal government designated the

Canadian as Canada's national horse. In 2009, this great breed made it onto a commemorative stamp.

Why these honours?

First is the breed's phenomenal war record. From the earliest days of settlement, the *Canadian* horse could be counted on. During the back-and-forth battles in the Ypres Salient during World War I, for example, *Canadians* could be found hauling food and ammunition to the front lines or artillery pieces in preparation for an assault, sinking belly-deep in mud and still grinding through. More than 325,000 Commonwealth horses perished during World War I. Thousands of *Canadians* were doubtless among them.

The second reason for these honours is that the *Canadian* was instrumental in settling Canada from the Maritimes to the Rocky Mountains.

Third, and perhaps most important, the *Canadian*, famous for patience and steadiness rare among its fellows, exemplifies the characteristics of the people of Canada themselves, showing endurance, strength, creativity and self-sufficiency in the face of great challenge and hardship.

FRONT-LINE MILITARY NURSING

In days long gone by, more soldiers died from disease and injuries due to lack of medical care than ever died in the heat of battle.

Throughout the many conflicts in the country's history, Canada's military medical services have developed to become among the most respected in the world. This is especially true of the nursing service.

The beginning of the nursing service was modest: four civilian volunteers who accompanied militia sent to quell the 1870 Northwest Rebellion. They were obliged to endure the same hardships along the trail as the troops and had the added challenge of treating injuries and illnesses that afflicted the men.

Their service proved to be immensely valuable, and the idea of incorporating a formal nursing service into Canada's fledgling military was born. With peace, the

Funeral of Nursing Sister G.M.M. Wake, who died of wounds received in a German air raid in France, May 1918.

idea lost steam as the militia slid back into hibernation.

Then in 1898, the country's military decided nursing support was once again required. When 200 volunteers were dispatched to the Yukon to help bring order during the gold rush, four members of the Victorian Order of Nurses were enlisted.

The trek to Dawson City took three months, living "rough" almost all of the way. The group had to cope with faint trails; dense bush; mountains; swamps; unnavigable rivers; wet and cold weather; air thick with insects; and a diet that required supplements of game.

The horses, mostly *Canadians*, were probably the only creatures on the trip that enjoyed it, and even they struggled despite being bred for such conditions. The troops, many of whom were city and rural lads out for adventure, experienced adventure and peril in equal parts, all of it from the terrain.

Delays were common. The column stalled while temporary bridges were built to cross rivers and logs were laid to support passage through swamps; advance parties searched out routes that might provide a river ford or meadows instead of impenetrable undergrowth; trees grew so closely together that wagons could not pass between them. The party also had to seek routes over, around, or between the mountains.

While there were delays, the nurses were not given a chance to rest. The march took a harsh physical toll on the troops as well, and without a doctor among them, the nurses were kept busy setting broken bones, binding sprains, suturing cuts, lancing blisters, diagnosing and treating sickness and supervising hygiene. At first sight, Dawson, no more than a filthy, primitive shanty town, must have seemed to the nurses and troops like a hub of civilization.

The 200 troops quickly settled into routine, relatively comfortable and uneventful garrison life. After all, their mission in Dawson was primarily "to wave the flag," and that's about all they did. As to law and order, the North West Mounted Police had these well in hand. But for the nurses, life here was a different story. Their work quickly extended into the town and nearby isolated villages, treating local people, many of whom had never experienced professional medical care.

The pace was exhausting; the equipment, medical supplies, and facilities inadequate; and the need seemingly never-ending. The nurses kept plugging away, and this fact was not lost on the military authorities. Soon there were fresh rumblings that the forces should have a permanent medical capability, at least with regard to nursing.

Matters were accelerated in 1899, when nurses accompanied the first Canadian contingents sent to South Africa to fight on behalf of Britain and the Commonwealth in the Boer War. Finally, in 1901, the inclusion of a nursing corps in the Canadian forces received a formal go-ahead. Of course, after the formalities, things continued to move slowly. It was 1904 before a small corps (25 nurses) was incorporated into Canada's reserve forces.

SAM STEELE: THE FIRST PEACEKEEPER

"Winning the heart and minds" of civilian populations in conflict areas seething with guerrilla and insurgent violence was not a strategy conceived by Americans during the Vietnam War.

Although he didn't use the phrase, this was exactly the strategy implemented during the last months of the Boer War by Sam Steele, a North West Mounted Police veteran and commander of Lord Strathcona's Horse. When the Horse returned to Canada, Steele stayed on, having been appointed a division commander in the South

African Constabulary and charged with cleaning out the last hard-core Boer resisters.

Steele knew from his policing experiences in western Canada and the Klondike that civilian co-operation and support were essential. To that end, he instructed his men in South Africa to provide non-military aid to Boer farmers.

The constabulary took over a variety of civil responsibilities, including licence issuing and census-taking, seemingly minor tasks but nevertheless critical to establishing order. They also acted as game wardens and veterinarians.

More important, Steele recruited Afrikaners into his ranks and encouraged the force to learn to speak Afrikaans. He lobbied hard and successfully to have Boer farmers given permission to once again possess firearms and arranged that some senior officers in the constabulary be appointed local magistrates. In short, he strove to instill confidence in the constabulary among local people. They were not an "occupation force"; rather, they were partners in civil restoration. Steele's efforts were seen by all as successful.

Steele's approach was again attempted by British Field Marshal Sir Gerald Templar during the 1948-1960 Malayan Emergency, though here its results were mixed. Templar recognized that "the shooting side of the business is only 25 per cent of the trouble, and the other 75 per cent lies in getting the people of the country behind us."

Steele and Templar's strategy paved the way as part of Canada's now traditional approach to peacekeeping and is still evident in Afghanistan. This is known as the 3-D approach – diplomacy, defence and development.

SNIPERS, THE VANGUARD OF SPECIAL FORCES

George Washington was once in the crosshairs of a British sniper, a lesser officer. The niceties of war in those days kept the sniper's finger off the trigger, though the shot could have stilled the American Revolution. Such niceties are no longer observed.

Artillery barrages, carpet bombing, roadside bombs, missiles and drones may seem to have changed the face of warfare in the past century, perhaps making the violence more impersonal. These methods could be seen as the sledgehammers of warfare. However, there are still scalpels. These are the snipers, selective because they have to be, covert, up close and personal because that's the only way they can be successful.

The first incidents of sniping occurred in the 17th century and were recorded because they were considered out-and-out murder. Those were days when warfare was more structured, even polite. Death from a distance was not considered good form.

During World War I, units of both sides relied on snipers to keep the opposition "honest." Officers particularly learned to keep their heads down and in some sectors, shaved off their moustaches and obscured the insignia that distinguished them from mere line troops.

The last Allied soldier killed in the First World War, Canadian Pte. George Price, died November 11, 1918, the victim of a sniper.

Before that, one Canadian soldier had made his mark as one of the premier snipers of the war. His name was Francis Pegahmagabow. He finished the war as Canada's most decorated aboriginal soldier, though he never rose above the rank of corporal.

Willing and Able

Cpl. Pegahmagabow enlisted in August 1914 with the 23rd Regiment (Northern Pioneers) and was among the first Canadian soldiers to enter the trenches of Europe. He saw action at the 2nd Battle of Ypres, the Somme, the Battle of Mount Soirel, Amiens, and Passchendaele.

As a sniper, Pegahmagabow is credited with 378 kills. He also captured 300 prisoners, many while on intelligence-gathering missions. His solitary scouting patrols across the lines and deep behind the German front provided invaluable intelligence, assisting in directing artillery and enabling more effective troop deployments.

Forerunner

Without realizing it, Pegahmagabow was defining the role of the modern-day sniper team — spotter, shooter, and sometimes backup man. Their missions still rely on stealth, patience, endurance and remarkable skill.

The missions themselves remain much the same — selective shooting, scouting, intelligence gathering, counter-sniping and, on occasion, kidnapping of belligerents.

No modern army is without its snipers. They now have weapons that are accurate well beyond 390 metres. They have at their disposal night-vision equipment, thermal imaging, laser and computerized rangefinders, miniaturized real-time data feeds, silencers and flash suppressors. And, especially in Afghanistan, some have had more challenging assignments — they must differentiate between civilians and belligerents.

Not all snipers survived. Because they were feared, because they were specific in their targeting and because they were covert, they were not treated as normal soldiers. Most often, if captured, they were summarily executed. Possessing a rifle equipped with a scope amounted to a death warrant.

Pegahmagabow did survive and after the war, he went home to his reserve. He was elected chief of the Ojibwa Parry Island Band in Ontario, following in the footsteps of his father and grandfather. Later, he became supreme chief of the Native Independent Government, one of the early forerunners of the Assembly of First Nations.

THE VICTORIA CROSS

The Victoria Cross is awarded "for the most conspicuous bravery, a daring or pre-eminent act of valour or self-sacrifice or extreme devotion to duty, in the presence of the enemy."

It is not awarded lightly.

Since 1856, the Victoria Cross has been the highest honour awarded a British Commonwealth member of the military for exceptional action in the field.

Military scholars routinely bicker over the actual numbers of Canadian Victoria Cross recipients. Veterans Affairs Canada includes several recipients on their list who, while born in Canada, emigrated to the British Isles while still toddlers. Another list includes Newfoundlanders whose service occurred before Newfoundland joined the Dominion of Canada in 1949.

Hairsplitting also extends to one case of a recipient born in the British Isles who served with the Ontario Provincial Police before returning to the British Isles to enlist in the British Army.

Despite these rather inconsequential kerfuffles in academia's ivory towers, one thing is not in dispute: the unquestionable valour of every recipient.

In 1993, Canada joined Australia and New Zealand in designating the country's own Victoria Cross. In 2003, Governor General Michaëlle Jean unveiled the new Canadian design for the award. It remains Canada's highest military honour.

The Victoria Cross

THE FIRST VICTORIA CROSS RECIPIENT

Lieut. Alexander Dunn travelled a long way from his birthplace in York to fight in the Crimean War. In 1854, he was in the Middle East, serving with the 11th Prince Albert's Own Regiment of Light Dragoons (Hussars), part of the British Army arrayed against the Russians and Turks.

The lieutenant's superb horsemanship and skill with a sabre would serve him well during the losing battle against the Russians. During the famous Charge of the Light Brigade, Dunn repeatedly charged forward against superior numbers to save the lives of other soldiers. Many dragoons had been unhorsed, and the Russians were hell-bent on finishing them. This made Dunn's task all the more daunting.

Dunn survived the Charge of the Light Brigade, only to die as a result of a hunting accident in 1868. He was buried at Serafa, a village in what is now Eritrea.

In 2001, Canadian peacekeepers from CFB Gagetown found his gravesite being used as a garbage dump. They cleared the area and built a cairn dedicated to his memory.

It was due to the uncommon bravery of this soldier, who was 21 when he fought in the Charge of the Light Brigade, that he became the first Canadian soldier to be awarded the Victoria Cross medal.

WILLIAM HALL: A CANADIAN SAILOR IN THE BRITISH NAVY

To this day, Avonport, Nova Scotia, honours Able Seaman William Hall, the first Canadian man of colour to be awarded the Victoria Cross.

Hall was the son of a rescued slave and a woman who fled Washington during the War of 1812. In 1842, in keeping with Nova Scotia's maritime tradition, he went to sea at the tender age of 15. Hall saw action with the U.S. Navy during the Mexican War and during the Crimean War with the Royal Navy.

In late 1857, Hall was part of a naval artillery brigade sent overland that was ordered to help relieve the Siege of Lucknow during the Indian Mutiny. Devastated by rebel fire, his battery reduced to one operable gun, Hall and Lieut. Thomas Young — the only two alive and unwounded — manned the gun under constant heavy fire long enough to create a breach for British infantry. Hall, as well as Young, received the Victoria Cross for this action.

Hall retired from the British Navy as a quartermaster in 1876, returning home to live with his two sisters in a small farmhouse near Hantsport. He was buried without military honours in a nearby churchyard, where his grave became neglected. In 1945, his body was disinterred and reburied in a special plot of land adjacent to the Baptist church in Hantsport, where a cairn was erected as a permanent memorial.

In February 2010, Canada Post released a stamp to celebrate the remarkable story of William Hall.

TIMOTHY O'HEA: THE ONE AND ONLY

In 1866, the Victoria Cross was awarded to Pte. Timothy O'Hea under circumstances so unusual they may never happen again.

Pte. Timothy O'Hea did not win his Victoria Cross in battle; nor was he a Canadian soldier.

O'Hea was an Irish soldier attached to the 1st Battalion, 1st Rifle Brigade. This unit of the British Army was stationed in Canada to defend against the

Timothy O'Hea. Private 1st Battalion Rifle Brigade.

Fenians, who were considered a very serious threat to the sovereignty of Upper and Lower Canada.

In June, 1866, O'Hea, along with four other brigade soldiers, was assigned to guard the rail shipment of 2000 pounds of ammunition. Hooked to the train were locked boxcars containing 800 German immigrants, including their families.

When the train stopped in Danville, Quebec, O'Hea spotted a fire in the ammunition car. The other four soldiers and the railway workers fled.

Single-handedly, the private bailed water from a nearby stream to quell the fire, making 19 trips back and forth for over an hour. He eventually climbed into the boxcar to tear apart wooden ammunition boxes and hurl the burning pieces clear. Meanwhile, the immigrants, unaware of their peril, cheered his efforts.

O'Hea's Victoria Cross has the particular distinction of being the only one awarded for an action on Canadian soil.

CHAPTER II:
A PLACE AT THE TABLE

In the years following the Boer War, political and military interests did not suspend operations while Canada created a viable armed force. Before there was much of an opportunity to take stock, Canada was agreeing to fulfil its obligation to the British Commonwealth and enter World War I. Canadians could not possibly have imagined what they were in for.

This was neither the Great War, except in terms of casualties, nor the War to End All Wars, despite being labelled both. Primarily, WWI advanced some of the military efficiencies, such as mechanization, that would characterize all future conflicts.

The first calls for volunteers to join the Canadian Army were enthusiastically over-subscribed. With minimal training, idealistic young recruits were transported to England for more training before consignment to the trenches in France and Belgium.

Finding ships to transport the recruits was difficult as the Royal Canadian Navy existed mostly on paper. Three top-line coastal Canadian Pacific Steamships had to be transformed into troop carriers.

To protect the West Coast against the threat of German battleships thought to be in the area, the premier of British Columbia had to broker a deal to buy two submarines, and these had no torpedoes or deck guns.

Canada also had no air force. Aspiring pilots first had to get to England, then join the Royal Air Force. Remarkably, two of the RAF's top aces turned out to be Canadians.

Canadians fought hard and fought well. Names such as Ypres, the Somme, Passchendaele, the Moreuil Woods and Vimy Ridge still carry profound meaning for Canadians. The casualty lists were long, and the loss of men and women profoundly impacted on thousands of families across the country.

Canadians particularly distinguished themselves when commanded by fellow Canadians. For this, they won a place at the signing of the Treaty of Versailles at the end of the war. Never again would Canada's military be the mere handmaid of another country.

A trench on the Canadian front showing "funk holes", France, 1917.
W.I. Castle / Canada. Dept. of National Defence / Library and Archives Canada / PA-001326

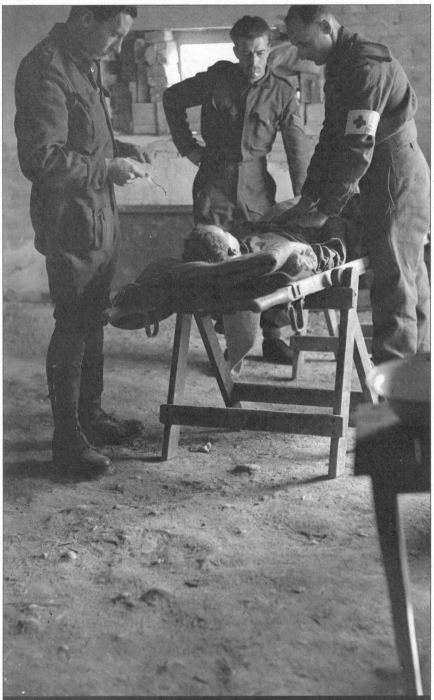

Personnel of the Royal Canadian Army Medical Corps checking the condition of a wounded Canadian soldier being evacuated to a Field Surgical Unit in Italy, January 15, 1944.

REMEMBERING JOHN MCCRAE

Military historians have used the century that has passed since World War I to autopsy every battle: the leaders, the politics, the weapons and lessons learned. Still, as the archived material and the memories become blurred by time, the war and its horrors are remembered with one blood red symbol, the poppy. Indeed, the poppy has come to symbolize the human losses of many wars.

The poppy's power to stir memory is attributable to a man whose short life was dedicated to saving lives rather than ending them: Canadian battle surgeon Lt.-Col. John McCrae, one of many thousands of people who did not survive that war.

Lt.-Col. John McCrae and his dog Bonneau.

Flanders, an area straddling the borders of Belgium, the Netherlands, and France, was the scene of some of the fiercest, most prolonged fighting in World War I, including the battles for Ypres and Passchendaele.

The 2nd Battle of Ypres, in 1915, was the first for Canadian troops, among them McCrae, who was in charge of a field hospital. With him, attached to the Canadian Field Artillery, was a close friend and former student, an engineer, Lieut. Alexis Helmer, all of 22 years old.

Helmer had enlisted in August 1914, following in the footsteps of his father, Brig. Gen. R.A. Helmer. Nine months later, Alexis was killed by artillery fire. Much affected, McCrae presided at his friend's brief burial service adjacent to the field hospital.

McCrae had already witnessed carnage, death and dismemberment on the battlefield, having first served in South Africa during the Boer War. Now, at 2nd Ypres, he saw that carnage expanded a thousandfold.

Still, the loss of his friend cut especially deep. His lament was intensified by the sight before him: poppies in full bloom around the field hospital and along the lanes, stark in counterpoint to the relentless din of artillery and acrid wafts of smoke and poison gas that tainted the country air.

During a lull, McCrae sat outside the surgery tent, within sight of his friend's makeshift grave, and wrote *In Flanders Fields*, a memorial for Helmer and for every fallen soldier.

In 1918, John McCrae died of meningitis, contracted at the front.

The poem was first published in the British periodical *Punch* later the same year, just as the general public was learning of the horrendous losses at 2nd Ypres. The expressive force of *In Flanders Fields* has resonated ever since.

IN FLANDERS FIELDS

In Flanders fields the poppies blow
Between the crosses, row on row,
That mark our place; and in the sky
The larks, still bravely singing, fly
Scarce heard amid the guns below.

We are the dead. Short days ago
We lived, felt dawn, saw sunset glow,
Loved and were loved, and now we lie
In Flanders fields.

Take up our quarrel with the foe:
To you from failing hands we throw
The torch; be yours to hold it high.
If ye break faith with us who die
We shall not sleep, though poppies grow
In Flanders Fields.

ARTHUR CURRIE: CANADA'S CITIZEN GENERAL

The British Empire was built as much on the force of arms as on economic ambition. By the dawn of the 20th century, the British military had a well established pecking order, both in its relations with Britain's colonies and also within its officer ranks.

Then, during World War I, a Canadian general would emerge who would effec-

General Currie, Commander of the Canadian troops in France and A.D.C.

tively shatter that pecking order. His name was Arthur Currie. Some have called him the greatest general of the war.

Within the pecking order, the colonies were expected to support any British military action without question. Britain still dictated the colonies' foreign policies, and colonial troops were expected to act under British command.

Colonial rank and file troops were generally held in low regard, almost treated as cannon fodder. Colonial officers, some of whom were professionals trained by the British, were obliged to toe the line. Still lower in the pecking order were reserve officers who were considered mere amateurs. One of those so-called amateurs was Arthur Currie.

In retrospect, suggests a former British officer, Currie's lack of military experience and formal officer's training may have been advantageous; he went to war without preconceived, often outdated notions of how to conduct warfare. He knew instinctively that strategies successfully employed by the likes of Napoleon wouldn't cut it along the trenches woven across France and Belgium.

Currie put a high price on life and possessed a fierce determination to preserve the lives of his soldiers, balking at throwing bodies after bodies in battle strategies. He risked court martial more than once in his refusal to sacrifice Canadian lives in what he considered futile endeavours.

Instead, Currie relied on meticulous planning and organization, a heightened level of training for troops under his command, confidence in and close communication with his junior officers. He trusted in his own stubbornness in the face of many British tactical proposals, and most of all, he trusted in his common sense.

The Canadian Way

The memorable Battle of Canal du Nord, in September 1918, was a clear case in point. Currie regarded the British plan as a summons to slaughter and insisted on implementing his own plan. The British saw this move as audacious and impractical but finally acquiesced, perhaps hoping Currie would be hoisted by his own petard.

Currie's plan called for a daring move across the dry section while engineers bridged the canal, and then for his forces to split, attacking behind the German positions to their left and taking Bourlon Wood to the right of the crossing.

Although the task of crossing the formidable obstacle of the Canal du Nord required expert planning and precisely organized artillery and engineering support, Currie's plan succeeded.

After the success at Canal du Nord came further wins at Vimy Ridge and Passchendaele.

Currie was a brilliant tactician who used his skills to reduce casualties and is credited with accelerating the end of the war. His slogan was said to be "Pay the price of victory in shells—not lives." Partly because of the noise and construction used in their advances, the four divisions that comprised Currie's 1st Canadian Corps were so effective the German's believed they faced at least 12 divisions.

By the end of the war, General Currie was knighted by King George V. Yet his return to Canada as the greatest general the country had produced was met with little fanfare. He took a post as head of McGill University and seemingly settled into comfortable civilian life, all of his battles fought and won.

Thank You, Now Go Away

But there was an issue that continued to plague Currie: the government's abysmal treatment of its World War I veterans. In 1929, when he stepped down as president of the Royal Canadian Legion, Currie didn't go quietly. He lambasted the Canada Pension Board, its bureaucrats and its regulations.

In Currie's view, and that of many veterans, the pension board was devoted more to obstructing the receipt of veterans' benefits than to providing them. His impassioned testimony, laced with many first-hand accounts, led to a hastily formed pension committee, whose members were given the job of bringing about some radical changes.

When it became apparent that the pension board's bureaucrats were hell-bent on stonewalling the changes, Currie once again took up the struggle. In the end, the new government of R.B. Bennett dismantled the board and replaced it.

More Than Just Another War

While many of Currie's contributions and those of the 1st Canadian Corps were certainly of tremendous immediate value to Canada, there is a long-term and more profound legacy to mention. Currie's implementations gave Canadian politicians the clout they needed to break the last significant colonial clutch the British had on Canada; control of the country's foreign policies.

The 1st Canadian Corps won Canada its independence on foreign battlefields. Canada was now strong enough to become a separate signatory to the Treaty of Versailles that officially ended the war. As well, Canada became a separate member of the League of Nations. This was tacit world recognition of the country's independence, finally confirmed in 1931 when the Statute of Westminster was passed by the British House of Commons.

Of this, Currie said, "Canadians have won their freedom by their own efforts and not because the Mother Country willed and wished it so to be."

" I would not wish to dignify warfare. I know too well that no pomp or circumstance, no waving of banners, can lend true dignity to war . . . . Those who have seen it and experienced it realize the horror of it, its frightful waste and extravagance."

– **Sir Arthur Currie**

MCBRIDE'S NAVY – EXECUTIVE DECISION

Sometimes the global military affairs of nations require a local touch to make sure they smoothly run their course.

When war was declared on August 4, 1914, Canada's West Coast was protected by only a few short-range coastal guns and a down-at-the-heels light cruiser, the *HMCS Rainbow*, based on Vancouver Island.

On the other side, known to be in the Pacific, was at least one ultra-modern German heavy cruiser — and maybe two — that could easily drop anchor outside the range of the coastal guns and systematically devastate the *HMCS Rainbow*, not to mention Victoria, Vancouver and the Nanaimo coal mines, for a start.

B.C. Premier Sir Richard McBride was well aware of his province's vulnerability from the sea. Until 1906, the might of the British Navy had protected Canada's shores, but she was at war now, her attention directed elsewhere.

Convoy carrying Canadian Expeditionary Force to Britain, October 8th, 1914.

The Royal Canadian Navy wasn't officially formed until 1910, and the government had not rushed to transform legislation into ships and sailors. The Royal Canadian Navy's total 1913-14 budget was barely $500,000.

McBride was understandably desperate but not without resources, one of which was having an ear to the ground. Days before war was declared, he picked up the rumour that two new submarines, originally commissioned by the Chilean Navy, were berthed at Seattle and might be for sale. McBride determined that one way or another, he would have those subs.

What McBride did not have was authority either from Ottawa or the province to buy submarines. At the 11th hour, he wrested federal funding approval, then cut a cheque drawn on the provincial treasury for $1.1 million. If Ottawa reneged on reimbursement, McBride's political career would be as dead in the water as his hopes, of course, for a navy. He might even end up in jail.

In the normal course of things, the acquisition would be a straightforward business deal between the province, the Canadian government, and the American shipyard that had built the submarines. These, however, were not normal times. As soon as Canada declared war, all sales of military material to Canada by American manufacturers were prohibited by the U.S. Neutrality Act. If McBride wanted the submarines, he would have to smuggle them to Canada. So he ordered just that.

The Game's Afoot

Late on the night of August 4, McBride's representatives departed Victoria Harbour on a nondescript coastal steamer. About 10 o'clock the same night, the two submarines slipped their mooring lines and, running on quiet electric motors, stole out of Seattle harbour. Their departure was clandestine — they had no official clearances.

The steamer rendezvoused with the submarines near Trial Island , in the Strait of Juan de Fuca, where McBride's people spent four hours inspecting the subs. Finally, the cheque was handed over, and under full power, the subs were rushed into Canadian waters and eventually into Victoria Harbour. *McBride's Navy* was born.

Two days later, the Canadian government repaid the province and the Royal Canadian Navy took over the subs, renaming them C1 and C2. That should have concluded the drama, but another problem arose — the submarines had no torpedoes.

Another night operation was mounted, and two Chilean practice torpedoes were purloined from the Seattle dockyard and spirited to Canada. The Americans beefed up their security following this second successful night raid, and while the Royal Canadian Navy officers pondered a third to obtain some vital innards for the torpedoes, they learned the same materials were en route from Halifax.

The two submarines, finally fitted for engagement, would uneventfully patrol Canada's Pacific coast for the next three years. As for *HMCS Rainbow*, she was dispatched on a hunt for the German heavy cruisers which, luckily for the seriously outgunned *Rainbow*, were already back in the Atlantic.

NO WHITE MAN'S WAR:
2ND CONSTRUCTION BATTALION

Even in wartime, old ideas can die hard. Some in command of Canada's military during the First World War considered it a "white man's war." The country's people of colour proved them wrong.

Up until 1916, black Canadians were not permitted to enlist in the armed forces. But by this time, the number of new volunteers was dwindling and casualties in Europe were mounting at a shocking rate. Expedience pressured Canadian Army brass to relent, and to accept black recruits.

On July 5, 1916, the Canadian Army officially formed the 2nd Construction Battalion, based at Pictou, Nova Scotia. Five hundred men of colour enlisted from Nova Scotia, more than 400 more came from Ontario, and 50 from western Canada. Potential recruits far exceeded the number required to fill the battalion's ranks.

Going overseas in 1917, the battalion's work was non-combative until the end of the war, although it was slated for action in the spring of 1918 on the Western Front. The battalion's contribution to the war effort involved construction of buildings, roads, bridges and airstrips — the support infrastructure vital for effective combat.

PASSCHENDAELE – HELL FOR ANY SOLDIER

Commander Arthur Currie angrily predicted that 16,000 Canadian soldiers would die in their two-week 1917 offensive against Passchendaele. Give or take a few hundred, his estimate was accurate.

Passchendaele was a small village near Ypres, Flanders. It had been the scene of fierce fighting in 1914 as British and French forces halted a German offensive there. Since then, fighting had settled into static trench warfare.

In April 1915, the Germans mounted a massive offensive against Ypres, and this time they used poison gas. This battle marked Canada's initiation into the war. Allied forces retreated around them, but the Canadians held their position and halted the German advance.

Another Allied offensive began in mid-July 1917, a two-week sustained artillery barrage that poured 4.3 million rounds onto German positions, followed by two

Final instructions before going into battle in France, October 1916.

million more rounds per week as the offensive tried to move forward.

Throughout August, September, and October, record rainfall deluged the area, severely slowing any advance. Long ago stripped of vegetation or shelter by years of artillery fire, the ground was a sea of mud, pocked with water-filled shell holes deep enough to drown wounded soldiers who often fell into them. Troop supplies could not get through; wounded could not be evacuated. The dead either rotted where they had fallen or sank into the mud, their bodies often providing the only near-solid footing for soldiers.

Canadians entered the line to relieve Australian troops in October. Cpl. Will Bird, 42nd Battalion (Royal Highlanders of Canada) saw in the Australians "men who looked like grisly discards of the battlefield, long unburied, who had risen and were in search of graves." Another Highlander in the 42nd remembered the stench, the "sour smell of disinfectants, stale gas, sodden clothing, and faint, sickly odours of decay." It constantly hovered over the battlefield, no matter which way the wind blew.

On October 26, the Canadians began their assault. The casualty rate was high. The 46th Battalion lost 70 per cent of its men. The 49th Battalion lost 75 per cent of its men on October 30 alone. But the Canadians fought on, taking concrete pill box machine-gun nests one at a time, capturing hundreds of Germans and killing or wounding thousands more.

Inch by inch, day by day, the Canadians persisted. Finally, on November 6, amid torrents of rain, the village of Passchendaele was captured. Not a single building was standing. The soldiers had fought across a wasteland to capture a wasteland, but every Canadian objective during the course of the offensive was taken.

Through the three months of fighting the Canadians established themselves as an elite fighting corps. By the end, nine soldiers received the Victoria Cross in recognition of their outstanding effort at Passchendaele, only one less than they were awarded during all of World War II.

BILLIE BARKER – THE LOVE OF FLYING

Born in Dauphin, Manitoba, Billie Barker spent his first year of World War I in the trenches as a machine-gunner. Then he started flying and became the most decorated flier of the war. Included among his honours was the Victoria Cross.

By October 1918, Barker was credited with shooting down 46 enemy planes. On October 27, he found himself flying alone over France when a German formation of 15 Fokker biplanes pounced on him from the clouds. Sustaining severe injuries in both legs and an elbow, he continued to fly while slipping in and out of consciousness.

Barker managed to shoot down four of the planes in this condition, bringing his total to 50. He crash-landed his tattered plane behind Canadian lines, where he was rescued. When Barker recovered sufficiently, he was awarded the Victoria Cross at Buckingham Palace.

Almost immediately after the war, from 1919 to 1922, Barker partnered with another Canadian flying ace and Victoria Cross winner, Billy Bishop, in Bishop-Barker Aeroplanes Ltd. Using confiscated Fokker aeroplanes, they performed aerobatics and mock dogfights at fairs and other public spectacles.

Following that short-lived venture, Lt.-Col. Barker was involved in establishing the Royal Canadian Air Force. On April 1, 1924, the official founding day of the RCAF, Barker was its acting director (1922-1924). Among the innovations he spearheaded was the regulation that all RCAF air crews must have parachutes.

THE ROYAL NEWFOUNDLAND AT SOMME: A GENERATION ON THE LINE

For Newfoundlanders, July 1st is not an easy day to celebrate Canada's birthday. It's the anniversary of the Battle of Somme, July 1, 1916, one of the bloodiest battles of WWI and one that robbed Newfoundland of a staggering percentage of its fighting men.

Although Newfoundland did not join Confederation until 1949, the island was a member of the Commonwealth, supporting the British efforts in both world wars.

In 1914, Newfoundland raised a full volunteer infantry regiment of 1,000 men,

Private Thomas Ricketts, V.C., 1st Battalion, The Royal Newfoundland Regiment.

the Royal Newfoundland Regiment, which faced its first action in September 1915 at Gallipoli. On the line for three months, they endured some of the worst circumstances that trench warfare had to offer. By the time the British withdrawal was complete in January 1916, the Royal Newfoundland had lost 40 soldiers.

Shocked by their defeat at Gallipoli, and with the war not going well on the Eastern Front, British commanders decided to redeem themselves in a massive summer offensive in 1916. This would be the Battle of the Somme, the largest battle of the war. Within this offensive, the Royal Newfoundlanders, 800-strong, would "go over the top" near the small town of Beaumont-Hamel.

The battle was fully engaged on July 1, but the Germans were ready for the charge. For the Newfoundlanders, the first harbinger of the horror to come was the delay encountered when they had to climb through piles of Allied bodies at the first line of British trenches. These men had not even made it as far as no man's land.

With each soldier lugging 66 pounds of bulky kit, the regiment pressed into the German machine-gun assault. The fruitlessness of the mission soon became obvious, and they had to retreat across the same field of bodies. Only 30 minutes had elapsed since they had left their trenches.

SGT. THOMAS RICKETTS, VC: A TEENAGE HERO

Thomas Ricketts, from White Bay, Newfoundland and Labrador, was not yet 16 when he joined the Royal Newfoundland Regiment to fight for the Commonwealth.

On Oct. 14, 1918, his platoon was being severely battered by machine-guns during an advance near Ledgehem. Armed with a Lewis gun, Pte. Ricketts and his section commander attempted to outflank the Germans' position but ran out of ammunition.

Ricketts backtracked under fire for more ammunition, then laid down such accurate cover-fire that his platoon was able to advance unharmed and capture four field guns, four machine-guns and eight prisoners.

Though he served long before Newfoundland joined Canada, Ricketts is considered the youngest "Canadian" to be awarded the Victoria Cross. Ricketts also received the Distinguished Conduct Medal and the Croix du Guerre.

In the end, the Battle of Somme would involve a million men. The Allied casualties exceeded 57,000, a great loss by any terms. But in sparsely populated Newfoundland, it was a rare home that was not immediately impacted by the destruction of the regiment.

At roll call the day after the battle, only 68 soldiers answered. The regiment had lost 710 men — dead, missing, or wounded, including every officer who had "gone over the top."

ORPINGTON, AN ATYPICAL OLDE ENGLISH TOWN

On the outskirts of London sits the quaint town of Orpington. Locally, the town is known for its Orpington hens, an annual gypsy convention and its crowning of a May Queen every year.

From a Canadian perspective, Orpington's finest hour began in 1915, when the government of Ontario donated $2 million to construct a 2,180-bed hospital there to be devoted to treating soldiers severely wounded on the Western Front.

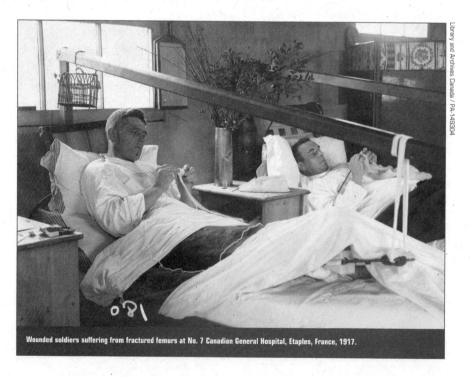

Wounded soldiers suffering from fractured femurs at No. 7 Canadian General Hospital, Etaples, France, 1917.

Canadian doctors and nurses treated more than 25,000 soldiers before departing for home in September 1919. By that time, the hospital (known as General Hospital No. 16) was providing state-of-the-art treatment, including occupational therapy for soldiers suffering from shell shock.

The hospital pushed medical frontiers in another direction as well, carrying out pioneering work in plastic surgery. Part of this ground-breaking effort was provided by Dr. Thomas McCrae, brother of Dr. John McCrea, who composed *In Flanders Fields*.

The services of the hospital were spectacular for its time. Only 182 of the seriously wounded soldiers that were admitted could not be saved.

Although #16 was demolished in the 1960s and replaced with a new hospital, the original is remembered in Orpington. One wing of the new Orpington General Hospital is named the Canada Wing and three wards are named Ontario, Quebec, and Mackenzie King, respectively.

Those patients who didn't make it are also remembered. A section of Orpington's All Saints Church cemetery is known as *Canadian Corner*, established for the interment of the 182 patients who died.

HALIFAX EXPLOSION

In 1917, as the war in Europe ground up men and material, Halifax, already one of the largest natural seaports in the world, was also the base for troops, munitions and other supplies destined for Europe from North America. Here the ship convoys were formed for the transatlantic crossing. Troops arrived by rail from all parts of Canada to be transported by ship overseas. Supply and munitions ships arriving from New York, Boston and Montreal clogged the harbour as they awaited inspection and clearance to join the convoys.

The threat of German submarines had resulted in antisubmarine measures at the mouth of the harbour. Harbour pilots had complained about the congestion for some time, and near collisions happened regularly. But for all intents and purposes, close calls don't count in wartime.

On the morning of December 6, 1917, the French freighter *Mont Blanc* entered the harbour to join a convoy heading east. The *Mont Blanc* was fully loaded with highly explosive munitions. Exiting the harbour at the same time was the *Imo*, a Norwegian ship heading to New York City. The two ships collided in the harbour's Narrows at 8:45 a.m., and the *Mont Blanc* caught fire.

The spectacle soon drew crowds to the dockside. Seamen from the *Mont Blanc* immediately abandoned their ship, rowed to shore and desperately tried to warn onlookers of their peril. By then, the benzol on the deck was afire. The *Mont Blanc* drifted to shore and collided with a pier. Then she exploded.

The blast was the largest wartime man-made explosion to that time, being surpassed only by the atom bombs of the Second World War. Every building within a square kilometre was instantly destroyed. Shock waves shattered windows, tore off roofs and collapsed walls a kilometre and a half from the harbour. People close to the blast's epicentre were vaporized.

Flood and fire followed closely. A 60 foot tsunami swept through the flattened city, sucking victims back into the harbour as it receded. Fires burned in the wreckage near the harbour and rapidly spread beyond. Both Halifax and Dartmouth, on the harbour's opposite shore, shared the same fate.

The substantial Canadian military presence in the city doubtless saved many lives, but with six square kilometres of Halifax reduced to rubble, their efforts, along with those of the fire and other rescue brigades, could not be enough. Of one extended family of 66 people, for example, only 20 survived. Mary Jean Jackson lost her 10 children, her husband, mother, four brothers, two sisters and several nieces and nephews.

The 20 to 25 minutes between the collision and the explosion was also long enough to draw onlookers to windows. When shock waves shattered the glass, many were permanently blinded. Still, the horror did not end.

While the blizzard that blew in on the following day, dumping 40 centimetres of snow onto the devastated city, did much to stifle the fires, it greatly hampered the efforts of rescuers digging for survivors in the rubble. With very little shelter available, weather took its own toll. Bodies were still being recovered the following spring.

On December 5, 1917, Halifax was a prosperous city. The war had injected it with life and bustle. By December 7, 1917, Halifax was a shattered, smouldering hulk, a casualty of the war.

Nearly 2,000 people died in the blast, the tsunami and collapsed buildings, 134 of them Canadian service personnel. Nine thousand more people were injured. Six thousand were now homeless, and another 25,000 were left with severely damaged houses.

GOOD TIMES, BAD TIMES, AND THE TAX MAN

World War I had an upside for many stay-at-home Canadians. The war effort brought booming economic times. But after the shocking casualty lists came the economic downturn that followed Armistice. The good times stopped rolling.

Apart from Canada's obligation to support Britain's military endeavours, the Canadian government had its own reasons for becoming active early in the war.

Canada's economy was in the dumps entering 1914. Grain prices, then the mainstay of the country's economy, were taking a beating due to crop failures and deflated world prices. Skyrocketing unemployment was exacerbated by a record

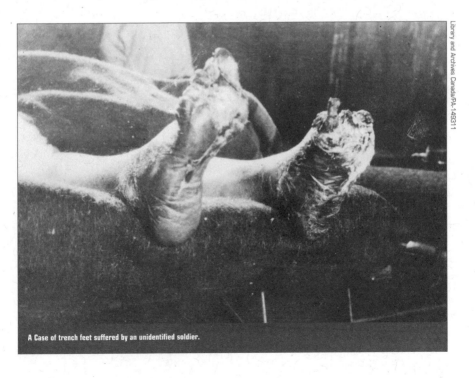

A Case of trench feet suffered by an unidentified soldier.

influx of immigrants, which began in 1910.

Unemployment was reduced as soon as the call went out for army volunteers. Not surprisingly, almost 70 per cent of those who enlisted in English Canada were recent British immigrants.

Enlistment in the military supplied the war machine and also turned around the economy. The country's manufacturing and service industries received a huge shot in the arm and soon surpassed agriculture as the primary source of the nation's wealth.

But there were growing pains, mostly due to patronage in providing contracts and profiteering in the provision of goods. Canadian soldiers suffered for it. Trench foot was commonplace on the front because substandard materials and workmanship meant that soldiers' boots rotted off their feet. The Canadian-manufactured Ross rifles jammed almost as often as they fired, and even then, their accuracy was dubious.

From 1916 to 1918, Canada thrived on full employment. The buoyant economy also enabled the government to pay for the war. Feeling patriotic, citizens readily accepted "sin taxes" on items such as alcohol and tobacco. For the first time, they also began paying what government called a "temporary" personal income tax. It proved to be not nearly as temporary as the economic boom.

As wartime demand for goods ended, rising inflation and unemployment beset the country. Many returning soldiers could not find work. Moreover, 1918-1919 was the period of the Great Influenza Epidemic, which seemed to target the country's fittest people, many of whom were veterans. The epidemic took as many as 50,000 lives in Canada. Between war and disease, Canada's death toll between 1914 and 1920 exceeded 110,000 people, carved mostly from one generation.

FREDERICK FISHER:
THE HERO FROM ST. CATHERINES

Due to his actions on April 22, 1915, St. Catharines, Ontario, native Lance-Cpl. Frederick Fisher became the first Canadian to be awarded the Victoria Cross during the First World War.

In 1915, Fisher was a machine-gunner with the 13th Battalion, Royal Canadian Highlanders Regiment, fighting near St. Julien in Belgium in the 2nd Battle of

Ypres. To protect regimental artillery from being overrun, Fisher crawled to a forward position and broke up a German advance. Of the six men accompanying him, four were killed.

The next day, while trying to set up a machine-gun to defend against German positions decimating his regiment ranks, Fisher was shot dead.

His Victoria Cross was awarded posthumously.

BISHOP AND BEURLING: THE KILLER B'S

Though wars apart, the "Killer Bs," air aces Billy Bishop and George (Buzz) Beurling, shared a singular passion – flying – and a singular distinction: Bishop was Canada's foremost combat air ace in World War I, and Beurling, Canada's best in World War II.

Billy Bishop, from Owen Sound, Ontario, was in his third year at Canada's Royal Military College when war broke out. In 1915, he arrived in England as part of a cavalry unit. But Bishop had no interest in horses or in modern trench warfare. He wanted to fly.

Captain William A. Bishop, V.C., Royal Flying Corps. Captain William A. Bishop, V.C., Royal Flying Corps.

Canada had no air force, so Bishop used social connections (he was married to the granddaughter of Timothy Eaton, founder of the Eaton's department stores) to talk his way into Britain's Royal Flying Corps. He flew first as an observer and artillery spotter. It was 1917 before he made it to France as a fighter pilot.

Within five weeks, he shot down 17 German planes. In June 1917, Bishop won the Victoria Cross, having single-handedly attacked a German air field, destroying two planes in the air and one on the ground. In a German pilot's zeal to get off the ground and engage Bishop, a fourth plane crashed into a tree.

By May 1918, when he was recalled to Canada to a hero's welcome, Bishop was credited with 72 kills.

With the outbreak of the World War II, Canada decided it needed its own air force; Bishop was appointed its air marshal in charge of recruitment.

Beurling

George (Buzz) Beurling, from Verdun, Que., was still a teenager when he earned himself a pilot's licence. He tried three times to enlist in the RCAF but was turned down each time because he lacked a high school diploma.

His passion prevailed. Beurling made his way to England, where he was accepted into the Royal Air Force. In September 1941, he received his wings. In July 1942, he was awarded the Distinguished Flying Medal. That September, he received a bar for it.

CANADIAN STEEL

Of the medal Beurling cherished most – the DFM – he said it was "the one gong that means something. You know what it means? It means all the time I spent trying to earn money for flying time to get a licence. It means that trip across Canada on the rods and the Seattle hoosegow and the long trek back. It means my attempts to get into the Canadian, Chinese and Finnish Air Forces and three trips across the Atlantic in a munitions ship to get into the RAF. It means all the months of training in England and the hell of a time I had to get posted to a front where I could get some fighting and prove to everybody else what I had known for years about myself."

Beurling was assigned to the Malta defence. Vastly outnumbered by the Luftwaffe every day, Beurling accounted for 29 kills as part of the skeleton force of Spitfires allotted to defend the tiny island. By the end of his war, he had a total score of 32.

Recognizing a Canadian hero when they had one, the RCAF now pursued Beurling and persuaded him to join up, using him to promote recruitment in a tour across the country. In his view, this was a waste of his time and expertise.

Beurling was 22 when he resigned from the RCAF. He tried the RAF again, but they wanted him to train pilots in tactics. He did manage to get some fighting time in, but Luftwaffe planes had become scarce. Beurling resigned from there too.

After the war in Europe ended, Beurling continued looking for another fight. For a time, he negotiated to join the Chinese against the Japanese, but that fell through. He married, and that fell through, too. On May 20, 1948, George (Buzz) Beurling, DSO, DFC, DFM and Bar, died in a plane crash in Rome as he took off for a flight to Israel, which at that time was fighting for its life as a new nation. He was 28 years old.

VIMY MEMORIAL: VISION OF A VICTORY

The drawn-out horrendous Battle of Vimy Ridge is considered by many historians to be Canada's greatest military victory.

In recognition of this achievement and the sacrifice made by Canadian military men and women at Vimy and, throughout France during World War I, the French government in 1922 ceded a square kilometre of land at Vimy to Canada for its use in perpetuity.

At this fitting location, Canadians decided to construct the most striking memorial to the country's casualties outside its own national boundaries in that war.

A design competition was conducted, attracting 160 submissions. Selected was the design of Walter Seymour Allward, Canada's foremost sculptor of Canadian military and civic memorials.

Work on the Vimy Memorial began in 1925, slowly and cautiously at first because the area was still cluttered with live munitions.

Central to Allward's vision were two massive limestone pylons rising 27 metres from their base. Once those were in place, the memorial began to take shape.

The Vimy Memorial.

Work got underway on 20 sculpted figures. The most prominent of these is carved from a 30-tonne block, the figure of a woman representing Canada and mourning its lost sons and daughters.

The memorial is at once solemn and majestic, speaking as much to hope as to sorrow. From the ridge where it stands, many of the 30 nearby cemeteries where Canadians soldiers are buried are visible.

In 1936, 11 years after Allward's masterwork was begun, King Edward VIII officially unveiled it.

In 2001, the Canadian government began an ambitious program to restore its 13 World War I battlefield memorials in Europe, mostly in France and Belgium. Eight of these were specifically Canadian, and the remaining five were for the Dominion of Newfoundland. The restoration of the Vimy Ridge Memorial was completed in April 2007.

The original plaster models of Allward's 20 figures are permanently displayed at the Canadian War Museum in Ottawa.

Canadian machine gunners dig in, Vimy Ridge.

THE LAST LAUGH

The Bedouins, nomads of the North African desert regions, have survived for centuries in their harsh environment not only because they have adapted to it, but also because they are resourceful and always have an eye open for the main chance.

In 1918, a 120-member Canadian army unit — mostly engineers, medical officers and nurses — on the Turkish Front (present-day Iraq) discovered Bedouins had another talent. They were skilled pilferers.

One night, an unknown number of enterprising Bedouins stole into the army camp, silently cut away the side of a tent and made off with the unit's mule harnesses.

Discovering the brazen theft the next morning, the Canadians were righteously indignant. Then outrage turned to laughter: the Bedouins had only donkeys; the mule harnesses wouldn't fit them.

Knowing the resourcefulness of the Bedouins, one soldier surmised that once the harnesses were found to be useless, they'd bring them back and try to negotiate a finder's fee. The soldier was wrong.

That night, the Bedouins crept back into the camp and stole the mules.

WINNIE THE POOH: STORY OF A MASCOT

The trapper wasn't waiting for a train. He was simply resting on a bench at the White River, Ontario, railway station. Leashed to the bench was a small black bear cub, which the trapper had brought out of the bush. The cub was an orphan; its twin and its mother having been killed. Leaving the cub on its own would have meant its certain death.

Lieut. Harry Colebourn, a Canadian Army veterinarian, happened to be travelling from Winnipeg to Valcartier on a troop and supply train. When the train made a stop at White River, the lieutenant hopped off to stretch his legs and, spotting the cub, got into conversation with the trapper. The lieutenant soon persuaded the trapper to sell him the cub for $20, then bundled it onto the train.

By the time the train pulled into Valcartier , the cub had endeared itself to both

Harry Colebourn and Winnie, 1914.

the soldiers and the train crew. Colebourn had given the cub the name Winnie, after Winnipeg, the home of many of the troops travelling with him that day.

Valcartier was the scene of the largest assemblage of Canadian soldiery in the country's young history. More than 20,000 recruits were training there as the Canadian Expeditionary Force in preparation for action on the front lines of France and Belgium.

On October 4, 1914, just a few weeks later, Colebourn and Winnie were shipboard headed for England. While the vet from the Prairies spent most of the voyage seasick in his bunk or with his woozy head drooped over the rail, Winnie took to the ocean like an old salt. She was a bubbly social butterfly, always on the lookout for a friendly face or a free snack.

After disembarking in Liverpool, Winnie travelled with the veterinary contingent to the CEF base on the Salisbury Plain. By now, she was a mascot extraordinaire, even appearing front and centre in formal Winnipeg Veterinary Corps photographs.

When the corps had to move on to the battlefronts in mainland Europe, Winnie couldn't make the trip. Colebourn found her a temporary home with the Royal Zoological Society at the London Zoo, intending to pick her up upon his return.

Although he visited her as frequently as possible during leaves, he decided not to take her back to Canada after the war. Winnie had settled nicely into her new digs. In no time she had become the zoo's most popular resident, a must-visit for every family that came through the gates.

Two of these visitors were children's book author A.A. Milne and his son, Christopher. Milne began to make up stories about Winnie for his son and finally put them into a book. In 1926, Winnie became Winnie the Pooh, history's most lovable fictional bear.

Winnie would live to be 20 and throughout her life never turned on a human, friend or stranger. She had her likes of course – condensed milk high on the list, as well-known to Londoners as Pooh's honey pot. Today, Winnie continues to be the official mascot of the Fort Garry Horse, Colebourn's original regiment before his transfer to the veterinary corps.

SIBERIAN SOJOURN

In late 1918, Canadian troops were shipped to Siberia. For these soldiers, Canada's war would not end that November 11. For many of these troops, it had only started.

Apart from the historic achievements of Canadian forces at Vimy Ridge and Passchendaele, 1917 was a bad year for the Allies.

Despite millions of casualties, the front in France and Belgium was stalemated; morale was at an all-time low. The French army mutinied, and to the south, the Italians were generally out of the war. In the east Lenin concluded the Treaty of Brest-Litvosk with the Central Powers (primarily Germany and Austria-Hungary), thus taking Russia out of the war.

Heading into 1918, civil war and anarchy still raged throughout Russia. Advancing southward with ease into this vacuum, Germany could occupy the Russian grain belt and elsewhere capture more than $1 billion worth of military materiel stockpiled in warehouses and on the docks of Vladivostok, Murmansk and Archangel. Perhaps with the latter in mind, Germany had already invaded Finland.

If successful, Germany would be able to divert troops to the Western Front and also resupply those already there. The Allies decided to send troops to Siberia to ensure the war materiel did not fall into German or Bolshevik hands. Britain called for Canada to provide the bulk of troops representing the Commonwealth.

Negotiations among the Allies as to the division of duties dragged into August 1918. Finally, matters were resolved, and recruitment began in Canada. The hope was to create the force with volunteers drawn in large part from veterans already returned from Europe. The effort failed, forcing the government to turn to conscripts, many of whom were French-Canadians already opposed to conscription.

The first Canadian contingent arrived in Vladivostok on October 26, 1918. Even after the Armistice on November 11 and well into December, Canada continued to send more troops, the government reasoning that war would continue with only the enemy changing, that is, from the Central Powers to the Bolsheviks.

The Canadians were based at Vladivostok, tasked, as far as they understood, to secure the stores of war materiel. From the onset, to the government's credit, the troops were not required to undertake any action except in defence of the stores.

Nevertheless, the Siberian winter was torturous. Frigid temperatures, interminable guard and patrol duties, poor living conditions, boredom and the knowledge that for every other Canadian soldier the war was over — these conditions haunted the soldiers throughout the deployment.

Finally, on April 22, 1919, the Canadian pullout began. The last Canadians arrived home in June. British, American and Japanese troops remained, the Americans and British into 1920 when support for the anti-Bolshevik forces collapsed.

The Canadian's Siberian sojourn hardly rates a comma in the postscript of the war, but it was part of the Allied "sojourn" that eventually culminated in the Cold War. It was, in many respects, the Cold War's first choosing of sides.

For the Canadian forces, the "sojourn" was significant because, despite both British and American pressure, Canadian commanders in the field refused repeatedly to involve their troops in offensive action, a strong indication of Canada's growing movement toward military independence.

VALOUR ROAD, WINNIPEG'S REAL MAIN STREET

To some, Portage Avenue and Main Street may be the most famous intersection in Winnipeg, but Portage and Valour Road in the city's west end has more going for it than a constant wind.

Until the First World War, Valour Road was Pine Street, a few blocks of inconspicuous bungalows and not many trees. Then, over the course of the war, three young soldiers who'd grown up on Pine Street were awarded Victoria Crosses for their selfless gallantry in separate actions.

The first Pine Street recipient was Sgt.-Maj. Frederick Hall of the 8th Battalion (Winnipeg Rifles), Canadian Expeditionary Force. He was honoured for successfully rescuing wounded comrades from no man's land during action at the Ypres Salient on April 15, 1915.

On September 9, 1916, Cpl. Leo Clarke of the 2nd Battalion, Canadian Expeditionary Force, chose fight over flight when he became separated from his unit during the Somme Offensive. After emptying his revolver against advancing Germans, he picked up abandoned German rifles and continued shooting, killing

Valour Road Monument.

five, wounding several and capturing one before the Germans retired. This individual action merited a Victoria Cross.

Lieut. Robert Shankland of the 43rd Battalion, Queen's Own Cameron Highlanders, Canadian Expeditionary Force, was the third Pine Street lad to receive the Victoria Cross. He was awarded the medal for leading a successful counterattack on October 17, 1917, retaking trenches lost at Bellevue Spur during the Passchendaele battles.

Hall and Clarke would be killed in action later in the war. Shankland would survive the war and eventually become a lieutenant-colonel, commanding the Cameroons.

In 1925, the City of Winnipeg officially changed the name of Pine Street to Valour Road in honour of these three soldiers and erected a small plaque at the corner of Valour and Portage.

CHAPTER III:
MILITARY INDEPENDENCE

World War II brought about enormous changes for Canada's military. For the first time in the country's history, it would march a full army into battle. Over the course of the war, the Royal Canadian Navy would grow to be the third-largest in the world. The Royal Canadian Air Force would become the fourth-largest in the world and would fly missions in every theatre of the war.

Canadians suffered disasters like the battles for Dieppe and Hong Kong, but also won great victories in Sicily, Italy, France and the Lowlands. From these campaigns, Canadians would add location names like Ortona, Juno Beach and the Scheldt to the list still resonating from World War I.

The soldiers were only the point of the spear. The shaft was made up of thousands of other contributors: engineers and construction battalions; medical personnel; drivers, mechanics, cooks, clerks — all essential parts to ensure the spear's point struck true.

On North Atlantic waters swarming with German U-boats, the Royal Canadian Navy shepherded merchant convoys carrying supplies to Europe. The convoys were manned by merchant mariners who, while not in the navy, faced the same treacherous sea, weather and threat from the enemy as the Royal Canadian Navy's escort destroyers and tiny corvettes tasked to protect them.

The casualty tolls on foreign battlefields rang in communities across Canada. Not a martial country, Canada's military support was given by need and obligation, not initiated by aggression. Nevertheless, the ability, tenacity and valour of its soldiers, sailors and fliers were unfailing. By war's end, Canada had taken a place as a world power, a military peer.

Corporal Urban Mayo, 13th Field Company, Royal Canadian Engineers (R.C.E.), Wyler, Germany, 9 February 1945.
Lieut. Michael M. Dean / Canada. Dept. of National Defence / Library and Archives Canada / PA-190816

PRELUDE TO PERIL

Adolf Hitler did not wait until World War II to change the face of warfare. He began in 1936, during the Spanish Civil War. Some 1,600 Canadians volunteered to fight in Spain against Hitler, Italian dictator Benito Mussolini and Spanish Gen. Francisco Franco, but first they had to fight their own government.

By 1936, Hitler was on a roll, having built Germany's military strength while being lionized by many of the political leaders of western democracies, including Canada and Britain.

When civil war broke out in Spain between the democratically elected government and a military junta led by Franco, Hitler opted to support Franco, supplying arms and troops. Communist dictator Joseph Stalin aligned Russia with the elected Spanish government.

For Hitler, the Spanish Civil War would be the testing ground for a theory: that shattering the will of civilians to support military actions could be as valuable as defeating an enemy on the battlefield. As well, Germany could field-test its new armaments and provide battle experience for its fledgling army and air force. Against this, Russia supplied the beleaguered Spanish government with outdated World War I weaponry.

Where There's a Will

With Russian support, Communist organizers throughout Europe, the United States and Canada began raising volunteers to fight in Spain. At this time, communism was viewed by many as the ultimate expression of democracy and had considerable cachet in Canada.

Between the impact of the Great Depression and drought across the Prairies, more than 30 per cent of Canadians were unemployed. Thousands of single, unemployed men were housed in so-called work camps while the government tried to figure out what to do. Any collective associations, even trade unions, were seen as a threat to established authority.

Despite government roadblocks, 1,600 Canadians were recruited by the Communist Party of Canada to fight in Spain. Of this number, only about a third were party members. The rest came from all walks of life. Some were veterans, some were idealists, some were adventurers and some simply wanted to do more than stagnate in the work camps. Contrary to press reports of the time, very few of the recruits were criminal types — thieves, drunkards, and such.

In all, 42,000 volunteers were recruited worldwide. They became known as the International Brigade. Within the brigade, many Canadians contrived to stick together. One such unit was the Mackenzie-Papineau contingent, the Mac-Paps as they became known. Their bravery in the face of state-of-the-art arms and professional soldiers became legendary.

In the Lines

The Canadian volunteers found conditions in Spain horrendous. Equipment, including arms, was in short supply, as was food. Training was negligible, and the weather was often vicious. At the Battle of Teruel in January 1938, Regina native William Beeching was sent to relieve a machine gunner only to find him dead, frozen to death in -18 C weather.

At Teruel, Canadians held the battle line for 20 days without relief and often without food. But Stalin's political commissars, attached to each unit, were focused on proper political education above all. Some Canadians were prosecuted for failing to adhere to the party line.

Canadians quickly became aware that there was a shortage of military leadership. The Spanish government's army had for the most part sided with Franco. Now there were more civilian politicians than professional soldiers running the show.

Renowned Canadian writer Hugh Garner recalled his experience at the battle for Jarama: *120 days in the trenches, bombarded by artillery and Stuka dive bombers, repelling wave after wave of infantry assaults. Ordered to "dig in" at Jarama, no one had a shovel; they had to use their knives.*

In the course of the battle, they also had to scavenge the weapons and ammunition of dead enemy soldiers to continue the fight.

NAME THESE TUNES

Canada's World War I Top 10 Golden Oldies

There may have been catchier tunes sung by troops in the trenches, sailors on the oceans, and folks waiting at home, but these have the distinction of being composed by Canadians.

The stuff of memories for a few and perhaps a path to remembrance for others, they convey Canadians' loyalty, sense of duty, loneliness, loss and optimism. Try matching the titles below to their first lines. (Answers in brackets).

Titles

1. Boys from Canada
2. By Order of the King
3. Canada, Fall In
4. God Bless our Empire
5. Goodbye Mother Dear
6. Good Luck to the Boys of the Allies
7. The Hearts of the World Love Canada
8. I'll Come Back to You
9. What the Deuce Do We Care for Kaiser Bill
10. There's a War in Europe

First Lines

a) It isn't enough to read the daily papers (3)
b) A soldier enlisted and to battle marched away (8)
c) The Empire's pride stands side by side (2)
d) Where, oh where, are the men of Canada (7)
e) The soldiers they were chatting as they left the old canteen (9)
f) Though England's foes may assail her (1)
g) A mother and her only son together sat one night (5)
h) Were you ever in a war zone, all you that laugh and play (10)
i) It's jolly good luck to Johnny Canuck (6)
j) There's an Empire whose dominions reach out North, South, East and West (4)

Canada's World War II Top 10 Golden Oldies

Title

1 Here Come the Boys of Canada

2. The Canadian and Respond long dash– Buy a Bond

3. When the Boys Come Marching Home

4. There'll Always Be An England

5. Let's Make A Job of It Now

6. Three Cheers for Churchill

7. 'Til the Lights of London Shine Again

8. We've Rolled Up the Old Umbrella (And Grabbed Our Old Tin Hat)

9. A Million Cheers for England

10. Land We Love

First Lines

a) More than 20 years ago Pappy went to fight the foe (5)

b) A million cheers for England, that rugged little isle (9)

c) Here was a man in Europe with a dream of mighty power (6)

d) There's an empire we love, thru' the wide world 'tis scattered (10)

e) Loving hearts will welcome back Johnny Doughboy, WAVE, and WAAC (3)

f) I give you a toast ladies and gentlemen (4)

g) Oh, a gentleman from England, he crossed the river Rhine (8)

h) Here come the boys of Canada (1)

i) Come buy your war bonds, don't delay (2)

j) Remember that last night we danced together in our Picadilly rendezvous (7)

World War II seemed to be the war when the music ended. Peacekeeping and "security actions" didn't seem to arouse much patriotic fervour or create a need for a lyrical escape from a defined enemy. Afghanistan has changed that. This conflict is a war by any definition, and its impact has awakened the nation. The music is emerging. We already have Bob Reid's Highway of Heroes. Then there's What a Soldier Left Behind, composed by Master Cpl. Elton Adams, part of a collection that dates to his deployments in Bosnia and Afghanistan. There will be more.

Home, Bittersweet Home

With defeat of the government inevitable, the International Brigade was ordered out of Spain. But the fight was not over for Canadians; crossing the border into France, they waited for repatriation. Meanwhile, in Ottawa, the RCMP made fierce arguments to deny them return, calling them a threat to the country.

Eventually, benefactors — including industrialist Garfield Weston — put up the money to bring them home. They recognized that these volunteers had fought for the democratic concept of the times. Though vilified by Canadian government officials, there were some citizens, like the 10,000 supporters who met them at Union Station, who considered them heroes.

In 1939, official Canada ceased to fawn over Hitler. Now the country was at war with Nazi Germany. Some veterans of the Mac-Paps and other International Brigade units enlisted to continue the fight. Others, who had opted to stay in Europe, became key personnel in Allied special operations in the occupied mainland.

Despite their contributions and the conditions that caused them to enlist in the first place, repatriated Canadian veterans of the Spanish Civil War were kept under RCMP surveillance until 1984. By then, most of them were over 70 years old.

THE PAL FROM GANDER

Before Newfoundlanders joined Canada, they had made great sacrifices to the Allied efforts in both world wars. During the second, one sacrifice was made by an exceptional Newfoundland dog named Pal.

Pal spent his puppyhood in Gander. He grew, as Newfoundland dogs do, becoming larger than a St. Bernard and much stronger. When Pal grew too big for his family, the Quebec-based Royal Rifles — on garrison duty in Gander — agreed to adopt him.

Pal was renamed Regimental Mascot Sgt. Gander and he shipped out with his regiment when they were deployed to Hong Kong. Here Gander became much more than a mascot. In the tragic debacle of Hong Kong, he was one of the regiment's most heroic defenders.

Infantrymen of C Company, Royal Rifles of Canada and their mascot en route to Hong Kong, 1941.

On a Hong Kong beach, Gander threw Japanese invaders into disarray when he assaulted them, barking and biting. Another time, he thwarted an advancing Japanese patrol near a small encampment of wounded soldiers.

The battle for Hong Kong was brief, one-sided and deadly. While Canadian contingents were overwhelmed, Gander seemed unable to accept defeat. During one assault, when Canadian forces could not raise their heads in the hail of fire, Gander watched a Japanese grenade soar into their position. He grabbed it in his teeth and ran off. Although Gander died, the soldiers of the Royal Regiment and Winnipeg Grenadiers lived to bear witness to his remarkable feat of valour.

In 2000, Gander was awarded the Dickens Medal, the most prestigious medal the Commonwealth bestows on an animal for combat heroism. This medal was the first to be awarded in 59 years and the first awarded to a Canadian animal.

BY THE NUMBERS

Numbers never tell the whole story. This is especially true of casualty figures. These tend to blur the reality, which is that they represent real Canadians – next-door neighbours, kinfolk, friends, fellow workers. They depersonalize the many ways to die and the pain of suffering in faraway places. For these reasons, numbers don't mean much to soldiers on active duty — they are the ones who must live with the daily reality.

BOER WAR
Number of Canadians enlisted: 7,000
Number dead: 224

WORLD WAR I
Number that joined the Canadian Army: 619,630
Number that joined Royal Canadian Navy: 5,468
Number that joined Royal Flying Corps (Canada had no air force): 24,095
Number that went overseas: 424,589
Number dead: 66,655
Number wounded: 172,950
Number missing: 11,285

Casualties
Ypres : 6,035 died
Vimy Ridge: 10,602 died
Somme: 24,029 died
Passchendaele: 16,000 died

WORLD WAR II
Number that joined the services, including 250,000 in RCAF and 50,000 women in various services: more than one million
Number dead: 44,893
Number wounded: 42,000
Number taken prisoner: 10,000

KOREAN WAR
Number that saw action: 26,791 saw action in Canadian Army
Number that saw action in the Royal Canadian Navy: 3,621
Number dead: 309
Number wounded or missing: 1,295

MEDICAL TREATMENT
World War I: 114 wounded per 1,000 died
World War II: 66 wounded per 1,000 died
Korean War : 34 wounded per 1,000 died

VIETNAM WAR
Number of Canadians (estimated) enlisted with American forces: 40,000
Number of known dead: 103

Because it is illegal under Canadian law for Canadians to enlist to fight other countries' wars, many enlistees used U.S. addresses when they joined. Others were immigrants from Canada to the U.S. who were drafted. About 10,000 more Canadians were enlisted than draft resisters who fled the U.S. to Canada (30,000 estimated).

GULF WAR
Number that saw action: 3,837 men and 237 women saw action; no reported casualties

These figures are repeated in final section
CANADIAN FORCES CURRENT STRENGTH (2008)
Land Forces: 19,500
Air Forces: 12,500
Naval Forces: 9,000
Support Services: 20,000
Reservists: 27,000

CADET CORPS
Royal Canadian Army Cadets: 21,000
Royal Canadian Air Cadets: 24,500
Royal Canadian Navy Cadets and Navy League Cadets: 15,000

SGT.-MAJ. JOHN OSBORN: TO THE LAST

John Osborn came to Canada shortly after World War I and was, in many ways, a typical British immigrant.

Osborn had served in the war with the Royal Naval Volunteer Reserve, seeing action at the Battle of Jutland. Originally a seaman, he took up farming on the Prairies after coming to Canada, then later worked for the Canadian Pacific Railway in Manitoba.

In 1933, he joined the Winnipeg Grenadiers, one of the two regiments fatefully shipped to Hong Kong in 1941. Soon after their landing, the Japanese struck with overwhelming force.

Within a few hours, Osborn's unit was fighting on its own, retreating and desperate. Osborn, sometimes alone, provided covering fire for his unit. As he moved back to a new position, he organized disoriented stragglers.

As he and his comrades continued to fall back, the remainder of his unit became surrounded, so closely that a hail of grenades fell upon them. Osborn grabbed and threw back all but one. This he smothered with his body, saving several lives by this action.

Valour in the face of certain defeat is an intense commitment to one's brothers in arms, brothers in one's charge. Osborn's actions were a powerful example of such courage and commitment.

CANADA'S SHAME: THE HONG KONG STORY

In 1941, Canada's government put in motion a series of events which would bring tragedy on more than 1,000 Canadian veterans and their families for over half a century. This is the Hong Kong story.

By late 1941, World War II was not going well for the British. Not only was Britain itself under siege by the Axis powers in Europe and North Africa, but its colonies in Asia were also facing a fast-rising military threat from Japan. In a gesture of support to Britain, the Canadian government offered troops to assist in the fortification of Hong Kong. The British quickly accepted.

THE SONG OF THE D-DAY DODGERS

Canadian troops battling their way through Italy were sore about missing the Big Show: the D-Day landings in France. For months, they had been fighting weather, terrain and some of Hitler's top divisions. Most Canadian units were undermanned due to casualties, and their public relations could not keep up with that of the Americans. They were feeling underrated and unappreciated.

But Canadians could still have a cynical laugh, as they did in their Song of the D-Day Dodgers, sung to the tune of Lili Marlene:

We are the D-Day Dodgers, out in Italy,
Always on the vino, always on the spree.
Eighth Army skivers and their tanks,
We go to war, in ties and slacks,
We are the D-Dodgers, in sunny Italy.

We fought into Agira, a holiday with pay;
Jerry brought his bands out to cheer us on our way,
Showed us the sights and gave us tea,
We all sang songs, the beer was free,
We are the D-Day Dodgers, in sunny Italy.

The Moro and Ortona were taken in our stride,
We didn't really fight there, we went there for the ride.
Sleeping 'til noon and playing games,
We live in Rome with lots of dames.
We are the D-Dodgers, in sunny Italy.

On our way to Florence, we had a lovely time,
We drove a bus from Rimini, right through the Gothic Line.
Then to Bologna we did go,
We all went swimming in the Po,
We are the D-Day Dodgers, in sunny Italy.

We hear the boys in France are going home on leave
After six months' service, such a shame they're not relieved.
We were told to carry on a few years,
Because our wives don't shed no tears,
We are the D-Day Dodgers, in sunny Italy.

We are the D-Day Dodgers, way out in Italy.
We're always tight, we cannot fight.
What bloody use are we?

Canadian and British prisoners of war, liberated by the boarding party from H.M.C.S. Prince Robert in Hong Kong, August 1945.

British intelligence had assured the Canadian government that Hong Kong could be easily defended, based on their estimate that only 5,000 Japanese troops were in the region. In fact, the Japanese had 50,000 troops in the region and had kept Hong Kong effectively surrounded since 1938. Moreover, these were troops that were battle-hardened by five years of war with the Chinese and supported by substantial sea and air power. Far from secure, Hong Kong would be indefensible if the Japanese chose to attack.

Ordered to Hong Kong were almost 2,000 troops and officers of the Winnipeg Grenadiers and Royal Rifles. They arrived November 16, 1941. The Canadian defence department had listed both units as "unfit for combat," which basically meant they were as yet untrained.

Some of the men had never fired a rifle at a practice range; their military experience until then had been limited to garrison duty, the Grenadiers in Jamaica and the Royal Rifles in Newfoundland. Such was the haste to get them to Hong Kong that much of their equipment was sidetracked.

Within three weeks of the Canadians' arrival in Hong Kong, the Japanese bombed Pearl Harbour. Over the next eight hours they also invaded Singapore, Guam, Wake Island, Malaysia *and* Hong Kong.

Prisoners of War

On Christmas Day, the British formally surrendered Hong Kong to the Japanese. The Canadian dead numbered 290; another 493 were wounded. And 1,685 Canadians were taken prisoner.

500 of these Canadians were imprisoned in Hong Kong. The other 1,185 were transported to Japan, where they were used for slave labour in mines and shipyards until their eventual liberation by the Americans 44 months later.

Throughout their imprisonment, the Canadians were subjected to starvation rations, physical abuse and almost every disease conceivably induced by over-crowding, poor sanitation and lack of medical treatment. In Hong Kong, 128 would die; in Japan another 136. The survivors would carry the physical and psychological scars of their imprisonment for the rest of their lives.

Shortly after the war, Japanese Lt.-Gen. Takoshi Sakai was hanged as a war criminal for atrocities committed by Japanese troops in Hong Kong, including the execution of wounded Canadian soldiers.

The Canadian government provided the Hong Kong survivors standard veterans' benefits upon their repatriation to Canada, though with some exclusions. The Hong Kong debacle, unlike that at Dieppe in 1942, had no saving grace. In the euphoria of victory, more people wanted it forgotten than remembered.

Redress

The Japanese government was the first to recognize that the torment of their Canadian prisoners of war from Hong Kong was extraordinary. In 1952, by way of redress, the Japanese paid each surviving veteran $1,344, (about $30 for each month of captivity). The Canadian government remained unresponsive.

In 1986, the War Amputations of Canada took up the cause of Hong Kong veterans, many of whom by that time had serious medical issues related to their ordeal. The War Amps made representations to the United Nations Human Rights Sub-Committee to seek additional redress from Japan. The Canadian government pointedly failed to support their petition.

The veterans continued to lobby fruitlessly, that is until the Canadian government began negotiating to compensate Japanese-Canadians interned here during the war. Simply put, the incongruity was insufferable for Hong Kong veterans.

Only in 1998 did the government acquiesce, at least a little. The government voted to provide $24,000 compensation to each still-living veteran and any living widow, of whom there were 400. The payment was provided "on humanitarian grounds," rather like charity, with not a whisper about culpability or more than 40 years of shabby treatment. In 1998, only 350 Hong Kong veterans were still alive.

REVEREND JOHN WEIR FOOTE: DUTY BOUND

If ever a Canadian wartime action could benefit from a chaplain, it was on the stony blood-soaked beaches of Dieppe on Aug. 19, 1942.

Rev. John Weir Foote, from Madoc, Ontario, was an honorary captain in the Canadian Chaplain Services attached to the Royal Hamilton Light Infantry.

Just after landing at Dieppe, Foote began working on the beach with the regimental aid station staff. For eight hours, he imperturbably walked through withering fire to reach wounded soldiers and help them to the aid station. Later, he would carry wounded to the landing craft for evacuation, under fire the whole time.

Finally, the battle lost, Foote refused a final opportunity to evacuate. He chose to stay with the remnants of the Royal Hamilton and was captured. Until May 1945, Foote remained a POW, continuing to minister to Dieppe survivors in the camp throughout those years.

Foote was an immovable rock in a whirlwind of fire and blood. The Victoria Cross was awarded not only for his actions at Dieppe but also for his unwavering commitment and example.

WITH HONOUR: HMCS RESTIGOUCHE

In 1932, the Royal Canadian Navy purchased a River-class destroyer from Britain's Royal Navy and commissioned her as HMCS Restigouche. Not much happened with her before 1939. but from then on her presence punctuated key moments in the Canada's efforts in World War II.

To the Royal Canadian Navy, she was just your average destroyer. To her crew, she was a bold, proud lady. Affectionately, the crew called her Rusty Guts.

A few lines describe her service record, and generally echo that of the other destroyers in the Royal Canadian Navy:

1939-40: Served as convoy escort in the North Sea and between Halifax and Plymouth. Participated in the evacuation of Dunkirk.

1941: Convoy escort service as part of the Newfoundland Command.

1943-44: Convoy escort service in the Mediterranean Sea, Bay of Biscay and mid-Atlantic at the height of the Battle of the Atlantic. Participated in the D-Day Normandy landings.

Post-VE Day(1945): For three months, used as troopship to bring home soldiers.

1946: Decommissioned and scrapped.

Time may have treated Rusty Guts cruelly, but she had character and a noble history. These qualities were remembered.

In 1958, HMCS Restigouche (2) was commissioned into the Royal Canadian Navy, the lead ship in her class. She would serve the Royal Canadian Navy and Canadian Forces for 36 years. In 1984, she, too, was decommissioned, but avoided the scrapyard. Seven years later, she was sunk to create an artificial reef near Acapulco, Mexico.

THE CHEAP AND NASTIES

Winston Churchill called Canada's corvettes "the cheap and nasties"— cheap because they didn't cost much to build and their crews were relatively small; nasties because despite their small size, they were effective as anti-submarine ships well-suited to supply convoys.

The Royal Canadian Navy personnel that crewed the corvettes called them "cheap and nasties," too, but for different reasons. Not an extra nickel had been spent toward crew comfort. They were so cramped the crew's mess doubled as their sleeping quarters, which meant one watch would often be eating while another was trying to sleep.

As for the "nasties," the corvettes were never still, tending to roll with every swell. They were never quiet; every sound was magnified throughout the lower decks — a wrench dropped in the engine room, a wave striking the bow, ice chunks flaking from the superstructure. The lower decks were unventilated, thick with humidity and slippery from constantly sweating pipes.

The first 10 Canadian-built corvettes were destined for the British navy in exchange for two new Tribal-class destroyers built in Britain. All 10 were crewed by Royal Canadian Navy sailors, even after the British took delivery, because the Royal Navy did not have enough manpower.

The Beginning of Legends

Few of the corvettes were fully equipped when they undertook their maiden voyages, but haste was essential. It was lucky none had the misfortune to encounter a German U-boat on the journey to Britain, because instead of the four-inch guns they were supposed to have, many had fake guns rigged from wood and canvas. On the HMS Windflower, the first commissioned corvette, the flagpole substituted for a gun barrel.

The Windflower's Canadian crew had to call on its ingenuity more than once. On one occasion, en route for Britain and alone in the mid-Atlantic, the Windflower blew a bearing in its single engine. Dead in the water, the ship was easy prey for any U-Boat that might chance upon it. Furthermore, the corvette, buffeted by the sea, was rolling so much that repairing the bearing

Stand easy in the stoker's mess of the corvette H.M.C.S. Kamsack.

was almost impossible.

Using every scrap of canvas available, including the crew's hammocks, a balloon jib sail was sewn together, which, when hoisted, kept the stern to the wind and minimized the ship's roll during the 27 hours required to repair the bearing.

From their introduction and throughout the war as convoy escorts, the corvettes were supremely valuable to the war effort. Royal Canadian Navy corvettes saw service in the St. Lawrence, the Atlantic and the Mediterranean. By the end of the war, more than 115 had been built, 112 named after Canadian communities. Ten were sunk during the war, seven by torpedo.

HALIFAX: THE CONVOY CITY

Whether its residents liked it or not— and often they didn't — the port city of Halifax has had a major place in Canada's military history since the days of the first settlements. Never was its role more vital than during the two world wars.

Throughout both wars, Halifax was North America's threshold to Europe. The city suffered grievously in 1917 when the Halifax Explosion levelled its core, killing and injuring thousands. By World War II, Halifax had rebuilt, though Haligonians may not have been ready for the new challenges and pressures thrust upon them.

In World War II, Halifax again became the staging port for the shipping convoys supplying the war effort overseas. Here all of the accoutrements of modern warfare were gathered and loaded onto merchant vessels for the transatlantic crossing, first to Newfoundland, then Iceland and, finally, the British Isles or the northern Russian port of Murmansk. Here, too, other cargo-laden ships from the eastern seaboard ports like New York City gathered to form convoys.

The Battle of the Atlantic was raging. Britain's civilian population was slowly being smothered by the Germans' incessant bombardment and their navy's cordon of U-boats. Britain looked to North America for food, clothing, medical supplies, and other necessities.

The Allied relief endeavour of World War II would mark the longest continuous effort attempted to that time. Much of it would be co-ordinated through Halifax, carried out in large part by the Royal Canadian Navy.

Halifax was the navy's most important base. Halifax Harbour berthed many of its escort destroyers and corvettes and was the location for its largest training facility. Vessels reported to Halifax shipyards for fittings and repairs.

HALIFAX: THE MOB RULES

Sometimes people just have to party. VE-Day in Halifax was one of those times.

Germany surrendered to the Allies on May 7, 1945. The Battle of the Atlantic had been won. In Canada, the official government announcement of victory in

Europe was to come late on the 7th, proclaiming the 8th a day of celebration. But, of course, the news leaked early to Halifax's military and civilian populations.

The city dreaded the possible celebratory response. Stores, restaurants and movie houses locked their doors. Liquor stores were closed, which many considered a provocation on a night of celebration, especially since Halifax had no legal drinking establishments.

There wasn't much left for carousers to do, not the citizens of Halifax nor the nearly 10,000 sailors, army, air force and merchant marine personnel stationed in the city. Throughout their time in Halifax, military personnel often had a tense relationship with the city and they chafed at the city's lack of services, notably its strong temperance stand. To eat in a restaurant or see a movie always meant waiting in long lines. To live off-base meant paying inflated rent, and to shop in the stores often meant paying exploitative prices that bordered on profiteering.

As crowds gathered, moderate civil disobedience escalated into a riot. Liquor stores were broken into and looted. Sailors were conspicuous by their uniforms, but civilians quickly swelled their ranks. The mob took over the downtown.

The rioting continued throughout the day and into the night. Attempts by authorities to quell the mayhem were overwhelmed. The job of controlling thousands of rioters fell to about 550 military and city police. Most of these probably had the skills to break up a bar fight, but none were ready for riot control.

THE DAMAGE REPORT FROM HALIFAX:

- 6,987 cases of beer, 1,225 cases of wine, 55,392 bottles of spirits looted from Halifax liquor commission stores

- 5,256 quarts of beer, 1,692 quarts of wine, 9,816 quarts of spirits looted from Dartmouth (across the harbour) liquor commission stores

- 30,516 quarts of beer "gifted" by Keith's Brewery

Source: Royal Commission of Inquiry, 1945

V-E Day riots in Halifax, N.S. at Grafton Park.

On May 8, official V-E Day, rioters picked up where they had left off. Added to that were several thousand sailors, granted leave to participate in official celebrations with the civilian population. The unofficial celebrations obviously had more appeal.

At the Keith's Brewery, the owner threw open the warehouse and gave the entire stock to the mob. This move saved the brewery from what could have been its destruction. The mob seemed grateful for the gift; according to one account, not a single window was broken, and the beer was shifted from the warehouse by an orderly line of willing hands.

By nightfall, the party was over. From a gang of thousands, police managed to charge 363 people, about half military and half civilians.

HALIFAX: ROUND TWO

In July of 1945, barely two months after the infamous V-E Day riots, the Royal Canadian Navy redeemed its reputation in the eyes of Haligonians by heroically averting a second Halifax Explosion.

A rush was on to disarm ships involved in the Battle of the Atlantic, with the result that the military main storage magazine in Bedford, at the north end of Halifax Harbour, was filled to capacity with live munitions. The surplus was piled on the surrounding jetties and any open outdoor space that was available.

On July 18, a barge crammed with ammunition was tied up at the main jetty. The barge exploded, scattering flaming debris over the area and starting numerous fires among the stacks of other munitions. Throughout the night, the sky over the harbour was lit by fire, and the air wracked by explosions.

Much of Halifax and Dartmouth were evacuated. People spent the night in fields and ditches or in parked cars removed from danger but close enough to watch the "fireworks" on the horizon.

At the centre of the action, where the largest fires licked at unexploded munitions stores, navy volunteers battled the fires into submission despite ammunition exploding all around them.

By dawn, the worst was over and the fires under control. The Royal Canadian Navy had prevailed. Grateful Haligonians were able to return to their homes, many in time for breakfast or, quite likely, for the cold suppers abandoned in haste the night before.

HMCS ATHABASKA – CANADA'S HARD-LUCK SHIP

Some ships should simply never put to sea. The Tribal-class HMCS Athabasca turned out to be one of these.

HMCS *Athabasca* was under construction in a British shipyard when it was struck by a German bomb. Despite this, work continued and soon, the ship was ready for sea trials. During trials, the ship was damaged during a ferocious North Sea storm and limped home.

An unidentified sailor checking the stowage of depth charges, January 1944.

When the Athabasca was readied for action, she headed into Scapa Flow in the Orkney Islands, where she promptly collided with another ship. After more repairs, she finally headed into the Bay of Biscay for anti-submarine duties. Here, in August 1943, she was struck by a glider bomb. The Athabasca again limped back to England for repairs.

In April 1944, while patrolling in the English Channel close to the French coast, the ship was torpedoed and sunk by a German U-boat. This time, there were serious human losses. The Athabasca's captain, Lt.- Cmdr. J.H. Stubbs, and 126 seamen were lost. Eighty-three surviving crew members were captured and spent the remainder of the war as POWs.

No other ship in the Royal Canadian Navy had endured quite so much hard luck.

THE PRINCES GO TO WAR

They couldn't possibly be as famous as the great ocean liners, the Queens Elizabeth and Mary;
Canada's offerings to the war effort were only princes – the Princes Robert, Henry and David,
but they did more than their part for the cause in WWII.

During the 1920s, cruising on richly appointed ships was as trendy as dancing
the Charleston and swallowing live goldfish. To compete on Pacific Coast routes,
Canadian National Steamships contracted the construction of three luxury cruise
ships, the *Princes Robert, Henry* and *David*. By the time the company finally got them
into operation in early 1930, the Depression had just taken hold. By 1935, the cruise
business was so bad the company lost money just by starting the ships' engines.

The war in Europe changed that. In 1940, the Royal Canadian Navy purchased
the three Princes for the war effort.

The *Prince Robert* was designated as an armed merchant cruiser, hastily armed
with obsolete World War I guns, and sent to provide transpacific escort duty. Late
in 1940, *Prince Robert* and her crew captured the German supply ship Weser just
outside the Mexican port of *Manzanilla*.

In 1942, the *Prince Robert* was pressed into service as a troop carrier. She was
the principal ship transporting the Winnipeg Grenadiers and 2nd Battalion Royal
Rifles to their fate in Hong Kong. The *Prince Robert* was back in Hong Kong 44
months later to pick up some of those same soldiers, survivors of persecution and
torture as POWs.

The *Prince Henry* and *Prince David* were outfitted as troop carriers and mother
ships for landing craft assault boats. On D-Day, they were two of the 110 ships
assembled off the Normandy beaches. Between them, the *Princes* landed nearly 800
troops on Juno Beach that day.

As the big war wound to victory for the Allies, civil war broke out in Greece.
The *Prince Henry* was part of an Allied flotilla that relieved the siege of Preveza,
assisting in the safe evacuation of 10,700 civilians and soldiers.

The three *Princes* were sold soon after the war. For a short time, the *Henry* was
used by the British as a troop carrier. In 1962, an Italian company bought her for
scrap. The cutting torches also caught up to the *Robert* that year.

The demise of the *David* came in 1951 after she developed major boiler problems while in Brazil. She was towed back to the British Isles where she was cannibalized for parts.

ICEBERG AHOY

During WWI, one of the unique ways to spot German U-boats was from planes catapulted off ships equipped with launchers. The big drawback for the pilots was that after a scouting mission, they had nowhere to land except on the water, where they had to hope a ship would pick them up before they drowned or succumbed to hypothermia.

As for the plane, only a ship equipped with a winch could retrieve it before it sank. The ship-plane conjunction may have seemed an oddball military idea, but it led to the eventual development of aircraft carriers.

Another oddball idea, that a mid-Atlantic iceberg could be used as an airstrip had been floated decades before World War II. Experiments in a London butcher shop's meat locker determined that a mixture of 14 per cent wood pulp and 86 per cent water could be frozen and shaped to withstand bullets, bombs and torpedoes. If only something could be done about the melting problem. Now, the British Admiralty and Prime Minister Winston Churchill decided a prototype was needed. This is where the Canadians came in.

Desperate Times, Desperate Measures

With the British footing the bill, Canada selected isolated Lake Patricia, near Jasper National Park, to construct a prototype. The military named it the *Habbakuk I*. The super-secret model was built on the ice in the winter of 1943.

With a wood frame, the model was 18 metres long, with a six-metre draft and nine-metre beam. It looked like a large wooden barracks. The workers, who had no idea what they were building, dubbed it Noah's Ark. The creation successfully withstood the spring thaw and, with the help of a small refrigeration unit, lasted well into the summer of 1944.

But some problems were encountered. First, the British wanted the "ship" to have mobility. Second was the size: they wanted the iceberg ship to be almost 12 metres and 600 metres long, enough to accommodate 150 bombers. To steer the creation, a rudder almost 30 metres high would be required, and to top off these ambitions, the British Navy decided the ship's range should be 11,000 kilometres.

The Canadian government had committed to 272,000 tonnes of pulp, 22,675 tonnes of insulation, 31.700 tonnes of wood, and 9,000 tonnes of steel (anything beyond that would seriously compromise Canada's overall war effort). But the Brits wanted more tests and a lot more material.

The curious idea was abandoned with the development of long-range bombers and mass-produced American aircraft carriers. Anti-submarine initiatives became more proficient as well.

Habbakuk I eventually sank, without fanfare or witness, to the bottom of Patricia Lake, where divers can still inspect its wooden skeleton.

SINO-CANADIAN SOLDIERING

During World War II, British Columbia's rugged interior was the site of more military activity than construction of an experimental warship made of ice.

In a super-secret camp overlooking Lake Okanagan, select groups of Chinese-Canadian troops were trained late in the war to conduct guerrilla attacks behind Japanese lines. Scattered across the countryside, these small groups were assigned by the British to take their skills to the jungles in Asia, where they would work with partisan and political groups to disrupt Japanese supply and communication lines.

Then, only days after the first Chinese-Canadians parachuted into the jungles, the bombing of Hiroshima and Nagasaki brought a swift end to the official war.

VJ-Day, the day of the Japanese surrender, did not have much meaning in many of the remote posts of the Asian war zones. The Chinese-Canadians, now given the mission of assisting the Allies in taking the Japanese surrender, encountered Japanese officers so cut off from their central command they didn't believe the war was over. They were not only reluctant to lay down their weapons but were ready to use them on the emissaries.

At the same time, partisan groups had to be restrained from exacting revenge against the Japanese. And political factions who had fought for the Allies in exchange for independence were finding that some European countries might not be as willing to let go of their colonial interests as they had promised.

Civil war across southeast Asia became a looming possibility as political factions jockeyed for power and the Allies jockeyed to retain their pre-war holdings, at least as political and economic spheres of influence.

Especially in Malaysia, the Chinese-Canadian troops were spread thin, sometimes having to work as individuals with only local partisans for support. Worn weary by disease and malnutrition, they held to their mission, rescuing starving Allied POWs and mediating between local factions to prevent military actions and civilian massacres.

Few in number but fierce in their loyalty, the Chinese-Canadians were eventually brought back to Canada, though with little fanfare. Indeed, the secrecy surrounding their recruitment and deployment had been so secure that most Canadians didn't know they had been in Asia.

LOYALTY REWARDED

For many Canadian blacks, the hardest fight during the war was not against the nation's enemies, but against the officialdom that discouraged their enlistment. Such was the difficulty confronting Sam Estwick.

Sam Estwick seemed to be the perfect recruit: young, fit, enthusiastic, a high school graduate with academic awards. But Estwick was black, an immigrant from Barbados who had come to Glace Bay, Nova Scotia, when he was four years old.

Estwick wanted to fly, and the RCAF was desperate for pilots and in full recruitment mode — just not for blacks. Estwick was flatly turned down.

Like many before him trying to face down the same rejection, he persisted, and eventually, his efforts paid off. The RCAF enlisted Estwick to train as a radar technician. He graduated first in his top-secret class and in late 1942, he was dispatched to England for advanced training. From there, he was sent to India to support the

Allies against the Japanese.

Airlifting supplies to beleaguered forces in the countryside was vital; the sea lanes were either closed or extremely hazardous, and the Japanese air forces were eager to pounce on supply planes.

The air route to China was over the Hump, the high Himalayas. There was a need for precision airdrops to guerrillas fighting in the dense jungles of Burma and Malaysia. With air guidance systems being so rudimentary, radar was absolutely indispensable.

Great technicians like Estwick made it happen. Serving on planes, ships, and sometimes on airstrips that had been hastily chopped out of the jungle, Estwick served his country with distinction. The RCAF was slowly coming of age.

THE INVASION OF NORTH AMERICA

During the grim days of 1941 and 1942, Canadians and Americans became well aware that the Axis powers, including Japan, would try to invade North America if they thought they had any chance of victory.

German U-Boats were attacking ships in the Gulf of St. Lawrence and down the Atlantic coast to the Caribbean Sea. Ships were being torpedoed within sight of the docks in major harbours like Halifax. In the Pacific, Japanese armies were sweeping through China and southeast Asia, closing in on Australia.

On December 7, 1941, the Japanese attacked Pearl Harbour, the main U.S. naval base in the Hawaiian Islands. Early the next year, they attacked and captured the Aleutian Islands of Attu and Kiska. The military of Canada and the United States saw this as a likely prelude to invasion on their own shores.

Canadian forces were operating under U.S. command for the first time. Flying from bases in Alaska, RCAF squadrons conducted anti-submarine and convoy escort missions. Further south, their missions also included long-range reconnaissance to provide early warning should the Japanese mount a carrier assault on the mainland similar to that at Pearl Harbour.

May and June 1942 were particularly tense. Several Japanese submarines were

Aircrew and groundcrew of No. 428 (Ghost) Squadron. August 18, 1944.

prowling off Washington state. Two merchant vessels were torpedoed, and there were two shore bombardments by submarine deck guns, one at Vancouver Island and one at the mouth of the Columbia River. Hampered by bad weather and the lack of air to surface radar, an extensive search for the submarines remained fruitless.

Weather would also be the villain in the worst tragedy to befall the RCAF in the Pacific. Seven RCAF Kittyhawks were en route to Umnak, a base in the Aleutians, to take back Kiska. Approaching in thick fog, five of the seven crashed into a cliff, killing all five pilots. The same fog bank enabled the Japanese on Kiska to escape.

The RCAF continued to participate in "softening-up" raids on Kiska before the infantry launchings. Returning from one of these missions, RCAF Squadron Leader Ken Boomer shot down a seaplane version of the dreaded Japanese Zero. This would be the sole enemy airplane destroyed by a Canadian Home Defence unit during the war.

Given the global scope of World War II, and because the potential threat to North America did not materialize, the North Pacific defence may seem a footnote in the war. But that threat was very real to the military men and women there, on 24-7 alert to defend against it.

PTE. ERNEST (SMOKEY) SMITH: BIG MAN IN A SMALL BATTLE

Like most natives of New Westminster on B.C.'s coast, Pte. Ernest (Smokey) Smith was accustomed to rain. The area gets so much rain, in fact, that the locals have learned to ignore it, and this is just what Smith and his fellow Seaforth Highlanders did at the Savio River in Italy, in October 1944.

The Seaforth Highlanders were ordered to cross the river and establish a bridge-head for the mechanized units following behind them. On the cold night of Oct. 21, with rain falling in sheets, they successfully made the crossing against stiff resistance from battle-hardened German defenders. But in five hours, the river had risen six feet, meaning that a bridge could not be thrown across the river. The battered Seaforths were pinned down but had to hold the position. Retreat was impossible.

Isolated, Smith's company faced three counterattacking tanks supported by two self-propelled guns and more than two dozen German infantrymen. Smith and his two-man crew took positions straddling a road when one of the crew became wounded. Smith knocked out one tank, then, standing in the middle of the road with a Tommy gun, beat back repeated infantry assaults before finally carrying his wounded comrade to safety. Smith then returned to his position and defended it until relief arrived.

For his action that night, Ernest Smith was awarded the Victoria Cross.

THE CANADIANS FACE OFF

They were called the D-Day Dodgers but in fact, if they hadn't been grinding down battle-hardened German troops in Italy, the D-Day landings in Normandy might have been a bust.

Canadian troops in Sicily and Italy were tasked with the taking of Italy, under the command of Gen. Bernard Montgomery's 8th Army. Sicily had been tough, but Italy was tougher. Many of Hitler's troops and artillery that had managed to escape Sicily made it to mainland Italy, reinforcing troops already dug in there.

Late in 1943, D-Day forces were already being mobilized in England. Regarding Italy, Hitler had a clear choice: he could give it up and move his forces to defend

Infantrymen of The Carleton and York Regiment preparing to lob a hand grenade into a sniper's hideout, Campochiaro, Italy, 23 October 1943.

the French coastline from the invasion attempt he knew was coming or he could stay and defend Italy. He chose the latter, and Canadians made him pay full fare.

The Italian Campaign

In the Italian Campaign, the Canadian 1st Army Corps fought as a unit for the first time in the war. They landed in southern Italy and slowly began to fight their way north. No objective was easy. Men saw friends die beside them and heard screams from the bowels of burning tanks. And all the time their valiant struggles for places like Rimini, Calabria and the Liri Valley were being overshadowed by the magnitude of the D-Day invasion. So, too, was the breakout from the Anzio beachhead, which closed the pincers on the Germans.

No Quarter Given, None Asked

Because of its location, the market and fishing town of Ortona was initially thought to have important strategic value, situated as it was on the eastern end of Hitler's Gustav Line, which stretched across Italy. As it turned out, it could have been bypassed. Simply reaching the town was a merciless struggle; two weeks of unrelenting battle to take crossroads leading to the town, finally secured by an assault of the Royal Canadian Regiment on December 19, 1943.

The Canadian advance into the actual town began the next day. The international press would dub the town *Little Stalingrad*. For troops on both sides, it became the stage for a ruthless contest of wills.

Streets and buildings were seeded with mines and booby traps. A booby trap in one house killed 24 members of the Loyal Edmonton Regiment. The lone survivor, Lance Cpl. Roy Boyd, was not pulled out of the rubble until three days later.

Buildings had been blown into the streets, blocking tanks and infantry from everywhere but where the Germans wanted them: the main street and the town square to which it led. Here, machine-gunners, mortar men and snipers were waiting for the Canadians.

In the streets, Canadian casualties mounted. There was no safe cover to be found. Canadians began "mouse-holing" from building to building. This meant blasting holes through walls in one building to get to the next, and this in a town built in Roman times, home to a pre-war population of 10,000 civilians.

No Lull

Christmas Day came, and the fighting continued. German paratroops, out of range in a railroad tunnel, shared candles and a few bags of oranges.

Throughout the day, Canadian troops were pulled from the fight for a Christmas dinner in the Church of Santa Maria di Constantinopoli. They had the good fortune to sit down to soup, pork, applesauce, cauliflower, mashed potatoes, gravy, oranges, apples, nuts, chocolate, mince pie, beer and cigarettes.

An organist played Silent Night, and soldiers had a few brief minutes to reflect. Some had died trying to reach the church for dinner. Others died on their way back to the fight. Still others refused to go to dinner — the path was too dangerous.

The Other Story

The Germans had been ordered to hold Ortona, primarily due to international media attention. The Canadian troops didn't know this, and nor did their commanders in the field. Finally, the Toronto Star declared the battle for Ortona won.

Actually, the previous night the Germans had quietly pulled out, ceding the town. At best, the battle had ended in a stalemate. The Germans would fight another day, far too late to salvage Europe from the Allies, or Italy from the 8th Army. The Canadians would win.

THE ORTONA TOAST

Tradition is a vital part of every regiment's history. Battles won, battles lost, no matter; the fallen, the forgotten and those carrying on must be hailed. At Ortona, the Royal Canadian Regiment did just that.

December 21, 1943, marked the 60th anniversary of the founding of the Royal Canadian Regiment. Still in the thick of the battle for Ortona, the Royal Canadian Regiment paused to give a brief but heartfelt toast to their warriors past and present. The command post was under fire, a fitting backdrop to the tribute made to Canadian will, strength and certainty.

Every officer knew this was not a good day. The battle had become a grinding down of both sides, and the regiment was woefully under-strength due to casualties. Forgotten was the anonymity of artillery and aerial bombing; Ortona was up close and personal – men killing other men with guns, bayonets, bare hands — anything, perhaps a brick picked up from the rubble. Doubtless, there was sadness and fear, but also there was faith in the rightness of the cause, faith in the regiment and the certainty of victory.

The beverage consumed in the Ortona toast on that December 21 was rum, water and a scoop or two of brown sugar, drunk from a white china mug. Some of the officers who shared the toast would die that day or shortly after, but *esprit de corps* held firm. The toast is now a regimental tradition, proposed every December 21.

Soldiers of the 3rd Canadian Infantry Brigade run into snipers and machine gun fire, Campochiaro, Italy, 23 October 1943.

Lieut. Alexander Mackenzie Stirton / Canada. Dept. National Defence / Library and Archives Canada / PA-129774

Tommy Prince (Centre) in Korea

PRINCE OF WARRIORS

Tommy Prince was no average soldier. By the end of the Second World War, he was Canada's most decorated soldier of First Nations descent. In itself, that made him exceptional, but Prince was more than a figurehead. He was one of the most feared members of the Devil's Brigade.

Tommy Prince, an Ojibwa from Manitoba, was first assigned to the Royal Canadian Engineers as a sapper. That didn't last long. He enrolled in parachute school, then volunteered to join the 1st Canadian Special Service Battalion, a somewhat secret unit formed in mid-1942.

As Prince would soon discover, the battalion was something more than a conventional paratrooper, reconnaissance or commando unit. It would be all of these, but also a combined American-Canadian commando unit that would employ new combat strategies with the utmost precision.

When the Americans issued a call for volunteers for the unit, they asked for experienced wilderness specialists — hunters, game wardens, lumberjacks and guides. Prince had grown up in the bush, had worked as a lumberjack and was an expert tracker, hunter and marksman.

Prince, along with 696 other Canadian soldiers, was posted to Helena, Montana, to join nearly 1,000 Americans with similar skills. There they underwent further training designed to make these tough soldiers tougher. Winter warfare techniques, hand-to-hand combat, mountaineering, amphibious entries, demolition, covert penetration and use of specialized weapons were all part of their no-holds-barred training, and it went on for nearly a year.

The unit's first mission was to Kiska in the Aleutians, where they arrived only to find the Japanese had already departed. Then, in December 1943, they arrived in Italy.

Just south of Cassino, the unit mounted its first mission against the Germans. After dark and in frigid temperatures, they scaled cliffs on ropes. Then, with silent penetration and ruthless efficiency, they overran a key German defensive position — the infamous Camino Ridge, from which death had rained down on British and American troops for weeks.

At Anzio, the unit fought without relief for 99 days. To escape their patrols, the Germans established their defensive line about a kilometre back from its original position, but the buffer zone didn't solve anything.

The Germans began calling them the Devil's Brigade, especially after soldiers began leaving stickers on dead Germans showing the unit's insignia and a comment in German, which, roughly translated, said "The worst is yet to come."

Prince excelled at lone reconnaissance missions, spending days and nights far behind enemy lines, gathering intelligence while living off the land.

In August 1944, his unit transferred from Italy to southern France before its formal disbandment in December of that year. At the disbandment ceremony, Prince was one of only a few of the remaining original Canadian members who got the salute from American troops.

In its short history, the Devil's Brigade accounted for 12,000 German casualties and took 7,000 prisoners.

Prince was called to Buckingham Palace, where King George VI presented him with the Military Medal for his achievements in Italy and the American Silver Star for gallantry.

The Devil's Brigade has a place in history other than its successes during WWII. Its training regimen and mission purposes were adapted by future special forces, including the Green Berets, SEALS, Delta Force and Canada's JTF2.

After the war, Prince became a vocal veterans' and natives' rights advocate, and, when the call came for volunteers for the Korean War, he joined the Princess Patricias from Winnipeg, the first contingent of Canadians to arrive in Korea.

TO HAVE AND HAVE NOT: ANTWERP

By mid-1944, the tide of war had dramatically shifted. The German forces had been run out of North Africa and the Mediterranean. They had been devastated deep in Russia, and the Russian army's offensive now rolled toward Germany. Canadian and American forces were advancing northward through Italy. Allied air power was relentlessly pounding the German heartland. In June, the Allies secured a foothold on the Normandy beaches and along Europe's northwest coast. On every battlefront, the Allied vise was tightening on Germany.

But the work was not finished, especially in the continental northwest. The

Allies required a major port through which to ship supplies. Without supplies, the advance would be stalled, possibly giving the Germans time to regroup. Antwerp seemed to suit the purpose, but the Germans were not going to give it up without a fight.

In early September, the Allies succeeded in capturing the city of Antwerp, but between the port and the sea lay the only access route, an 80-kilometre stretch of the Scheldt River, still firmly controlled by the Germans, who had had four years to construct their defences, and the geography was much better suited to defence than to assault.

Apart from three islands forming an isthmus, which split the river's wide mouth, much of the land along the banks was below sea level, protected by dykes which also served as the only roads. The 1st Canadian Army Corp was assigned to decipher this challenge and capture the section of river.

Corp commander Lt.-Gen. Guy Simonds called in air strikes to destroy the dykes and flood some of the lowlands. Then, on October 2, 1944, he committed his ground troops to the assault. It would be one of the most fiercely fought battles of the war.

Just to obtain access to the Isthmus required two weeks of unabated fighting. On October 13, the Black Watch took 175 casualties and lost all of its officers, but three days later, the combined weight of the Royal Hamilton Light Infantry, the 10th Armoured Regiment and all of the division's artillery was thrown against the defenders. The Corp succeeded.

The last German stronghold on the Scheldt, Walcheren Island, was the most formidable. The only access was a narrow 12-kilometre causeway. Canadian troops of the Black Watch, Calgary Highlanders, and Regiment de Maisonneuve managed to secure a foothold and hang on until relieved by British troops. Fighting continued until November 7, when all that was left was the mopping up.

The first supply ship, HMCS Fort Cataraqui, docked at Antwerp on November 28, 1944. The Canadian army had moved on.

IN WAR AND PEACE

Eedson (Tommy) Burns was not a soldier's soldier or an inspirational general. While he was in command of the 1ˢᵗ Canadian Army Corps, fighting in Italy, troops dubbed him Laughing Boy and Smiling Sunray because of his sour and standoffish demeanour. But in his way, he was a champion to the Canadian cause.

Burns was a professional career officer, schooled at the Royal Military College and an instructor for a time. His combat experience began in 1916. He was wounded twice in France, receiving the Military Cross for his actions during the Battle of the Somme. He was also an officer in the trenches during the Canadian victory at Vimy Ridge. Later, he would serve as Gen. Henry Crerar's right-hand man, helping to prepare Canadian troops for the battles of World War II.

A Pen as Powerful as a Sword

Burns was a writer, too, contributing regularly to the *Canadian Defence Quarterly* and the famous *American Mercury*. These periodicals were platforms for his views of the military, in particular his opinions about the pivotal importance of armoured capability and employment.

Writing in 1935, Burns was critical of the Canadian and British military's failure to think in terms of armour and air power in modern warfare. German involvement in the Spanish Civil War and the lightning speed of the German blitzkrieg clearly backed up his arguments.

Such views did not endear him to old-school military leaders accustomed to static trench warfare. They also bristled at him during WW II when he complained that Canadian troops were used as cannon fodder in ill-conceived, under-equipped forays dreamed up by strategists far removed from the battlefield.

And Burns had been there. During the eight months in which Burns commanded the 1ˢᵗ Canadian Corps, his troops "went further and faster than any other corps," not easy in the Italian theatre's war of attrition.

The Germans had so much respect for Canadian troops, acquired during two world wars, that whenever they learned Canadians were coming into a battle sector, they immediately strengthened their positions or made plans to withdraw. Still,

Lieutenant-General E.L.M. "Tommy" Burns.

Burns's superiors believed he wasn't doing enough, or they said so at least.

Considering his squabbles with the Allies' military establishment, having a personality that didn't exactly light up the officers' mess or a war room and his reluctance to commit his troops helter-skelter, Burns's dismissal from the 1st Canadian Corps after only eight months as its commander was inevitable. He was shuffled off to a position behind the lines.

Doing It His Way

After WWII, Burns joined the Department of Veterans Affairs, serving as deputy minister between 1950 and 1954. Here again, his lack of charm and his abrasive drive to have things done his way weren't always appreciated.

Throughout his military career, his way meant the way that was best for his constituents; first soldiers and now veterans. His daughter was quoted as saying that Burns "dressed in seedy clothes to find out how his department treated veterans, and, unhappy with what he learned, raised hell."

His Biggest Challenge

In 1954, Burns was appointed to command United Nations peacekeeping forces in the Middle East, tasked with attempting to keep the lid on aggression between Israel and opposing Egypt, Syria, Jordan, Lebanon and an assortment of Palestinian groups.

Burns had no illusion that UN efforts would lead to sustained peace; none of the belligerents was interested in laying down their arms. Peacekeepers, whose weapons were limited to sidearms, were spread thin along the borders and they were mostly unwelcome.

While in the Middle East, Burns took the trouble to learn Arabic in order to handle mediations. He was accused of anti-Semitism for not learning Hebrew and was obliged to explain that as Israeli negotiators were fluent in English, French, or German, there was no need for him to learn Hebrew.

But Burns hadn't come to the Middle East to make friends. He undertook the job to protect Canadian political and economic interests in the region, which included supporting NATO. These were the years at the height of Cold War tensions; the potential for increased Russian influence in the Middle East was of high consideration in the West.

By persistent and patient negotiation, Burns was able to establish buffer zones and observation posts along the borders. His model would become characteristic of future UN operations in other conflicts. Indeed, this model would propel Lester Pearson to the achievement of a Nobel Peace Prize, shortly after which he became prime minister.

Burns spent five years as the Middle East UN commander, returning to Canada in 1959. After that, he drifted into obscurity, very much a forgotten and underrated soldier. To those who care to remember, Burns is considered to have proven himself a first-rate field commander, administrator, teacher, writer, advocate and peacekeeper.

CHAPTER IV:
NEED TO KNOW

TALKING THE TALK

Canada's military men and women are versed in many languages. Nevertheless, they have created a language that is uniquely their own. A Berlitz Guide to Canadian Forces would probably include some of these:

The most genteel term for military police may be *Red Hats*, referring to their distinctive red berets. Navy shore patrol members are sometimes known as *Crushers* and in the army, they're known as *Meatheads* or *Thunder Chickens*, referring to the thunderbird on their badges.

By any name, if they nab someone on the road of malfeasance, they may eventually deliver him up for a stretch at *Club Ed*, the Edmonton Detention Centre, Canada's main military prison.

Reservists are probably the most luckless when it comes to nicknames. Not only are they *Weekend Warriors*, they are also *Rentals* and *Saturday* or *Sunday Soldiers*.

Nor does SAS refer to the elite British equivalent to Canada's JTF2, our *Secret Squirrels*. Rather, it refers to reservists' Saturday and summer duty. Then there's *SWAT*, meaning some weekends and Thursdays, and *Toons*, shortened from cartoons seen only on weekends or, whenever seen, still not real.

Officers in all services have their own crosses to bear. Some are *Whistleheads*, recognizable because they stand around whistling with their hands in their pockets or — as they say — *wearing their American gloves* while troops work. Officers who go strictly by the book are known as *Pussers*. Others may be *OPIs* – only person interested. Some OPIs are said to lead by their well-developed *Loudership*, the talent for leading by screaming.

Martial music and military ceremony go a long way to defining public perception of the Canadian Forces, but around the parade ground, the rehearsal hall, so

Private A.R. Quinn, Princess Patricia's Canadian Light Infantry (P.P.C.L.I.), with captured accordion in Gambarie, Italy, September 1943.
Lieut. Terry F. Rowe / Dept. of National Defence / Library and Archives Canada / PA-115155

to speak, musicians are sometimes called. *Tune Techs* or *Tuba Techs*, *Bandies* or *Band Geeks*; their practice area is Tune Town, which, of course, makes the leading officer the *Mayor of Tune Town*.

HEAD OFFICE

The *Puzzle Palace, Cowering Inferno* or, as some call it, *Disneyland on the Rideau*, refers to National Defence Headquarters in downtown Ottawa, and assignment there is *Capital Punishment*.

Canadian Forces personnel also have names for most of the main bases in Canada. Petawawa, for example, is the *Chicken Ranch*. CFB Alert Bay is sometimes known as Home for the *Frozen Chosen*, though the term applies to almost any thoroughly inhospitable base in the country. Then there's *Gagtown* for Gagetown in New Brunswick and *Valcatraz* for Valcartier in Quebec. The Meaford, Ontario, base is known as *Mudford* and is reputed to have a *weather machine*, an infernal top-secret military device that guarantees lousy weather even while the rest of the world is bathed in sunshine.

TRADEMARKS

Few of the trades in the military manage to get by with their official names. Paratroopers are known as *Lawn Darts, Green Lights* or *Meat Bombs*. On the other hand, a paratrooper is apt to term anyone who is not a paratrooper a *Leg*, meaning, "lacks enough guts."

Infantrymen never have it easy; *Ground Pounder* and *Gravel Technician* are not derogatory terms to them; they're statements about their operational reality. *Cement Head* is not so nice. Soldiers in the armoured units call them *Crunchies*, presumably for the sound heard when a tank runs over them. There are more:

Twenty-mile Sniper — artillery gunner

Thumper Heads — field engineer

Super Stoker — specifically trained marine engineers

Spark Chaser — avionics technician

Shitter Fitter — naval hull technician

Zoomie — air operations member

Bin Rats, Blanket Stackers, Box Kickers — all are supply technicians

Circus Battalion — service battalion (erects tents and staffed by Clowns)

Combat Florist — anyone in Signal Corps; sometimes called Siggies

Dozers — aviation technicians

Gun Plumber— weapons technician; sometimes called Knuckle Dragger

Line Ape — lineman in Signal Corps

Metal Bashers — aircraft structure technician

Paperclips — members of Logistics Branch

Rubber Head — communicator research operator

The navy also has a few terms that might elude the average person. The navy itself is the *YMCA*; a sailor is a *Boat Person* or *Guppy*. Leading Seamen are sometimes known as *Killicks*, meaning spare anchors. Boatswains are *Deck Apes*; *Sliders* are navy personnel adept at disappearing before a full watch is completed.

The air force seems to have escaped lightly, known mostly as the *Chairforce*. More derisively, its members are also know as *Canaries*, too pretty to shoot, too yellow to fight.

CUISINE

Every soldier since the first one in history, even pre-history, has something to say about the food they eat and the folks who put it together. The Canadian Forces are no different.

Some cooks are *Chemists* because they simply have to keep on tinkering with whatever they prepare. Others are known as *Fitters* and *Turners*, the cooks who fit everything at hand into a pot and turn it into s---. Either way, personnel sometimes advise each other to hit the chow line wearing their *Bunny Suits* — chemical warfare defence outfits.

As for the food itself, salvaging some menus are *Fat Pills*, also known as *Jim*

Booglies and *Licky Chewies* — the dessert items. Usually the field rations, pre-packaged individual meal packs, or IMPs, contain these, but distaste for some IMPs has inspired the term *I Must Puke*. One such IMP, the infamous alleged omelette in mushroom sauce is known as *Lung in a Bag*. Another version of the IMP, the meal ready to eat (MRE), is also known as *Meal Rejected by Ethopians*. Nevertheless, few in the military would be caught without their *Gut Wrenches*, their cutlery.

STANDARD ISSUE

Equipment and issue uniforms have inspired some creative terms. The C7 rifle is known as a Bang Stick; the newer C7A2 comes equipped with the *Crocker Cocker,* a fragile cocking handle latch so obtrusive it can snag on a cobweb. Machine-guns are generally known as Pigs because of their voracious appetite for ammunition. Combat safety glasses are considered so ugly they're referred to as *Birth Control Glasses*.

Some old hands suspect that the H.J. Heinz Co. had a contract to supply the Clothe the Soldier Program with uniforms in the '90s. The term they use for standard issues is the *Relish Suit*. Other personnel call these their *You Can't See Me Suits*. Maybe that's not so bad. The old uniforms were called *Green Pyjamas*. As for boots, they're *Black Cadillacs*. Running shoes are *Silver Bullets*. Because swimming is an important part of basic training, swim trunks are standard issue. They're called *Grape Smugglers*.

GETTING PERSONAL

Some military personnel, orders and operations naturally invite unofficial names. *5 By 5* means everything is working OK. *Snafu*, however, means Situation Normal All F****** Up. The latter can often result in a spin- doctoring effort known as *DAC-A*, Deny Accuse Counter-Accuse. Alternatively, if ignored, a *BOHICA* can occur – Bend Over, Here It Comes Again. Just as bad could be a *TEWL*, a Tactical Exercise Without Leaders. It doesn't refer to abandonment but to poor leadership.

Among more onerous functions for officers are endless lectures and briefings. The worst are termed *Death By PowerPoint*. One way to avoid some of these is to *Voluntold* a representative of lower rank. In this case, voluntary attendance is sug-

YOU KNOW YOU'RE IN
THE CANADIAN FORCES WHEN

- You discover other countries have more poisonous snakes and carnivorous creepy crawlies than your own.

- You've had to wear forest green battle dress in a desert and vice versa.

- You're never told where you're going or what you're supposed to do until you get there.

- American beer tastes better than none at all.

- The "pause that refreshes" is two hours of sleep in a slit trench.

- What's written on the mess menu has no relationship to what's heaped on your tray.

- Initiative can get you a medal or a demotion.

- There's no fight attendant on the plane.

- You've been vaccinated for everything except what you catch.

- A day of rest really means a 32-kilometre full-pack hike in uncharted wilderness.

- Water tastes better than whiskey.

- You know there are fundamental differences between the army, navy and air force even when you're told there isn't.

- You can carry on a conversation using only acronyms for nouns.

- You finish cold-weather training just in time to be ordered to the equator.

- You can't remember the reasons for all of the ribbons on your dress uniform.

- When you say, "Been there, done that," you really have.

- You get to ride free on Via Rail every summer.

- You're posted to countries that aren't on any map.

- You get home from your rotation just in time to say goodbye to your wife as she starts hers.

gested but the tacit meaning is that the so-called volunteer damn well better show up.

Among the less-than-endearing terms is *Chuggernuts*, which has been around since the Second World War at least, and means stupid person. *Numpty* has a similar meaning. A more contemporary term for these unfortunates is Glue Bag. Keeners are soldiers who enthusiastically holler *HUA* and pitch in to any task, no matter how idiotic or useless it may be. However, when most soldiers holler HUA, it's used ironically.

In any military environment, personnel will strive to maintain some kernel of individuality. In early militia days, this wasn't difficult; no one had a uniform except certain officers, and they had to buy their own. Today, most soldiers still have a *Gucci Kit*, a few items they've acquired outside normal issue. Then there's the LCF, the Look Cool Factor, like switching an issue boonie cap for a Tilley. Of course, perhaps the most permanent *LCF* is a tattoo – a little ink can make quite a statement!

MILITARY SHORTHAND

The Canadian Forces is a complex organization, which at times may seem to be constructed of acronyms used to conduct its business. Every branch and operation — from the Department of National Defence Headquarters in Ottawa to units active in the many countries where Canadians serve — is often described by an acronym.

Some are official. For example, speaking of "official," there's ACOL, which stands for Area Co-ordinators of Official Languages. Canada has perhaps the only ACOL in the armed forces of the world.

One acronym that might stump the average infantryman is DQOL. That's the Director of the Quality of Life. A soldier trying to build a snow shelter during a blizzard on his first night of arctic survival training would probably like his DQOL's name, if not the home address.

Some acronyms indicate a lot of respect. A SME (Subject Matter Expert) pronounced Shmee, can save lives because he's not only BTDT (Been There, Done That) but has also passed all the relevant academic courses and training.

A SME might be called in to brief a unit about to go outside the wire to FISH, a high stress, high risk assignment, such as many encounter in Afghanistan. This isn't sitting by a stream dangling a line while watching the sun go down; FISH means Fighting in Someone's House.

Some acronyms are misnomers. One that stands out is BTU. This acronym emerged in the '90s, when the Canadian Forces obtained newly designed uniforms from the skin out. It means Brassiere Temperate Underwear. We're more familiar with the British Thermal Unit (also BTU). The Canadian Forces use of this acronym stands for Basic Thermal Underwear.

Lower ranks in every branch of the military might suspect there is a desk jockey somewhere at headquarters whose responsibility is to create acronyms for every facet of military life. But it is in the lower ranks that creativity truly reigns. Well-crafted acronyms acquire new descriptions, officers acquire nicknames, job descriptions acquire new meanings.

Some terms have found their way into common usage but most remain exclusive to the military. Knowing a few of these can go a long way toward understanding a conversation among members and veterans of the services. As for others, they're OSs (that's official secrets to you).

REGIMENTAL NICKNAMES

Regiments are the heart of Canadian land forces. They hold the history and the pride of their soldiers. Still, they have not escaped being tagged with sometimes irreverent, even profane, nicknames, some proudly accepted and defended by regiment members, others that stir some ire.

Right off the top, some regimental nicknames can't make it in this family reading book. Notwithstanding, here's some of the others that pass with at worst a PG rating.

Name	Nickname
5th Field Regiment. RCA	Five Tribe
7th Toronto Regiment	7 Guns
12th Regiment blinde du Canada	12th Rubber Boot Company
1st Hussars	1st Hosers
48th Highlanders of Canada	The Glamour Boys

48th Highlanders of Canada	The Dirty Four Dozen
8th Canadian Hussars – Princess Louise's	The Crazy Eights
Algonquin Regiment	The Algoons (WW II)
Algonquin Regiment	The Gonks (current)
Argyll & Sutherland Highlanders of Canada (Princess Louise's)	Ash Cans
Brockville Rifles	The Brocks or Broken Rifles
Calgary Highlanders	Calgary Highgranders
Canadian Grenadier Guards	Canadian Girl Guides
Canadian Grenadier Guards	Can't Get Girls
Essex & Kent Scottish	Eeks and Squeaks
Fort Garry Horse	The Garrys
Governor General's Foot Guards	GooGooFooGoos
Governor General's Horse Guards	Gugga Huggas
Grey & Simcoe Foresters	Farmer Johns
Grey & Simcoe Foresters	The Gay and Simple Farmers
Hasting & Prince Edward Regiment	Hasty Ps or Hasty Preedies
King's Own Calgary Regiment	Kay Ohs
Lincoln & Welland Regiment	Lincs or Lincs and Winks

Lord Strathcona's Horse (Royal Canadians)	Lady Strathcona's Riding Club
Lorne Scots (Peel, Dufferin and Halton) Regiment	The Forlorn Scots
Loyal Edmonton Regiment (4th Battalion, Princess Patricia's Canadian Light Infantry	The Loyal Eds or Eddies
Queen's Own Rifles of Canada	Queen's Own Rentals
Royal 22nd Regiment	Vandoos or Les Vingt-Deux
Royal Canadian Dragoons	RCD's
Royal Canadian Regiment	Royals or Run Chicken Run
Royal Canadian Regiment	Rocking Chair Rangers
Royal Hamilton Light Infantry (Wentworth Regiment)	Riley's
Royal Regina Rifles	Regina's or Farmer John's
Royal Westminster Regiment	Westies
Royal Winnipeg Rifles	Little Black Devils
Seaforth Highlanders of Canada	Seaforth or Bullwinkles
South Alberta Light Horse	Sally Horse or Sally Ho
Stormont, Dundas & Glengarry Highlanders	Glens or Sand, Dust & Gravel
Toronto Scottish Regiment	Trot Scots
West Nova Scotia Regiment	West Novas

THE PRINCESS PATRICIA'S CANADIAN LIGHT INFANTRY HAS REAPED A HOST OF NICKNAMES:

The Pats
Princess Pats
Patricias
Picklies
and Ping Pong Champs of Long Island

Chapter V:

Peacekeeping, Peacemaking and Police Action

Between 1914 and the end of 1945, Canadian military forces spent 10 years fighting in the two most destructive wars in history. Now, Canadians wanted lasting peace and security.

Canada's Lester B. Pearson was credited with designing an international police force to help resolve the 1956 Suez Crisis. He received the 1957 Nobel Peace Prize for his efforts. In effect, this proved to be the UN's first designated peacekeeping mission.

Pearson, who became prime minister just after receiving the Nobel, took the position that since Canada proposed the idea, it should always be the first country to commit its military to peacekeeping. Over the years, the Canadian military and the term peacekeeping have become synonymous.

However, since the first days in the Middle East and Cyprus, Canada's activities in this arena have become far more diverse than patrolling, observation and mediation. The expanded role came to include foreign aid supply, security and support; security for development workers and medical teams; construction; and training of local security forces and civil administrations.

Canadian forces discovered that there was often precious little about peacekeeping that was peaceful. They were regularly in harm's way, hugely outnumbered, facing heavy arms and automatic weapons with only their sidearms, all the while constrained by the UN's rules of engagement, which confined the use of force to self-defence in life-threatening situations.

The fundamental shift from relatively benign peacekeeping to aggressive enforcement began to surface during the civil war in Yugoslavia, where a force of

Master Corporal Shaun Burdeyny, a member of the Provincial Reconstruction Team Patrol Company, at Camp Nathan Smith in Kandahar, Afghanistan.

arms was eventually required to rein in horrific violence and ethnic cleansing. This type of presence was required again in the Gulf War.

Concurrent with these actions, peacekeepers continued to work in other countries throughout the world, particularly in support of famine relief, local infrastructure development, and local training.

THE PRICE OF PEACE

Cyprus is one of the most picturesque islands in the Mediterranean Sea. Members of the Canadian Forces know it well; it's now mandatory procedure to send Canadian soldiers to Cyprus to decompress after a rotation in Afghanistan. But in 1974, Cyprus was a place where Canadian soldiers died trying to keep peace.

Canadian troops first arrived in Cyprus in March 1964 as part of a UN mission to maintain peace between Greek and Turkish Cypriots. The effort dramatically broke down in 1974, when the Greek Cypriot National Guard staged a coup d'état with the intention of making Cyprus a part of Greece.

Five days after the coup, the Turkish army, supported by its air force, landed an invasion force of 30,000 troops on the island. The battle was on, and very quickly, UN peacekeepers began to take casualties. Within eight months, nine peacekeepers were killed and 62 wounded. This included three Canadian dead and 18 wounded.

The peacekeepers tried to evacuate civilians from the battle zones, often having to use confrontation tactics to get them to safety. On numerous occasions, the UN forces and their encampments were deliberately fired upon by both sides.

On August 2, the Canadian force was joined by troops from its Airborne Regiment and reinforced with a variety of heavier weapons and 16 armoured personnel carriers.

On August 14, Finnish peacekeepers came under a major Turkish air, mortar and artillery assault. Under constant fire from the air, the Canadian Airborne used the newly arrived armoured personnel carriers to evacuate the 117-member Finnish contingent. Adding to the challenge, Turkish commanders demanded that

Canadian Peacekeeping in Bosnia.

the UN forces protect Turkish Cypriot civilians during these attacks.

Three Canadian Forces fatalities occurred in separate incidents. Airborne Paratrooper J.L. Gilbert Perron was shot while sitting in a jeep on August 6, likely by Turks.

On September 10, Paratrooper J.J.C. Berger was shot by a Greek Cypriot guardsman while on a humanitarian mission.

On April 1, 1975, RCR Capt. Ian Patton was shot on the balcony of his hotel, probably by a guardsman, while taping a letter to his wife.

The Canadian Forces contributed to peacekeeping on Cyprus until 1993.

COLD WAR IN THE ARCTIC

From the late '40s to the mid-'60s, print media expended a lot of ink describing the heating up of the Cold War. What received very little attention was an arena of the Cold War that never heated up: the Canadian Arctic.

The imminent threat of another world war, this one nuclear, was taken very seriously by western powers. Jointly, American, British and Canadian military planners went so far as to draw up detailed defence strategies against Soviet aggression.

On April 29, 1949, Russia detonated its first nuclear device, and westerners were duly alarmed. Schoolchildren practiced nuclear air raid drills, which mostly involved crouching under their desks away from windows; backyard bomb shelters were popular enough to be a value-added selling point for house realtors. The Canadian government was sufficiently distressed that it built several nuclear-proof bomb shelters for government and military leaders.

The Coldest Front

Despite this security-conscious burst of construction, the real action was in the Arctic, and it was already in high gear as early as 1946, beginning with Operation Muskox.

Before Muskox there had been no significant military presence in the Canadian Arctic; the Canadian Army had no winterized equipment or clothing suitable for

I AM CANADIAN . . .

Cpl. Conrad Cowan, Somalia.

- I wear combats, not fatigues and I work for a "lef-tenant," not a "loo-tenant."
- I drive an Iltis, not a Jeep or a Humvee, and the weapon I carry for my protection is a C7, not an M16.
- I observe from, or take cover in, a trench and not a foxhole.
- I don't just speak English or French, nor am I bilingual. I can speak many languages.
- Although I am trained to fight in a war, I don't cause them.
- When I am not deployed on a mission of peace, I travel all my country, fighting forest fires, battling floods, rescuing lost souls or repairing damaged caused by an ice storm.
- I try not to take sides and believe in treating all humanity equally.
- I don't just go on patrols. I also clear land mines to make the area safe for everyone.
- In my off-duty hours while deployed, I occupy myself by rebuilding schools or playgrounds and I teach children in a wartorn country about peace and harmony.
- I am my country's best ambassador and I am respected the world over for what I do best.
- I carry my country's flag shamelessly and hold my head up high wherever I go.

My name is Frank, and I am ... a proud Canadian peacekeeper.

Master Cpl. Frank Misztal

Credit: Jenifer Borda. War and Peacekeeping. Canadian Heritage Collections. Rubicon Education Inc. 2002.

this environment. Even after the gruelling experience of winter in northern Italy and the devastation wrought on German troops by the Russian cold, it took the Soviet threat to inspire the army to act. Muskox was to be a challenging test of innovative material and techniques.

The Royal Canadian Air Force had just as big a challenge on its hands, due to lack of infrastructure. The air force would have to supply Muskox from temporary airfields and by airdrops, and it would also be relied on to chart access routes for the ground parties, though sudden weather changes continually altered the landscape.

The operation's main ground party consisted of 48 Canadian Army officers and men, plus four observers — three from the U.S. military and one from the Royal Canadian Navy. The group set out from Churchill, Manitoba, on February 15, 1946, travelling in 12 enclosed snowmobiles equipped with tracks.

On March 15, they reached Cambridge Bay, the most northerly point of their trek, then turned south to Coppermine and Port Radium. They crossed Great Bear Lake in April, slowed by pressure ridges in the ice that made passage extremely perilous. One four-tonne snowmobile went through the ice, as did a bulldozer sent to free it. The bulldozer operator died in the attempt.

Not All Ice and Snow

As the party moved southward, spring thawing turned trails into rivers of mud. Advance engineers and sappers were flown in to bridge rivers and streams swollen by spring runoff. Hastily built rafts made perilous crossings of waterways choked with debris from flash floods. The last leg of the 5,000-kilometre journey had to be made by rail; the snowmobiles were beyond repair.

Operation Muskox demonstrated the extreme difficulty of land operations in the Arctic. In addition to the 48 army personnel on the ground, more than 200 others were required to provide support. However, the RCAF, flying 1.3 million kilometres and dropping 380 tonnes of cargo with pinpoint accuracy in the barrens, had indisputably proved its value.

The role of the RCAF in the Arctic would become even more critical as the Cold War intensified.

Corporal Jill Cooper, Canadian Forces Support Unit (Ottawa) Photo Services, DND SU2005-0466-51a

The Avro Lancaster Bomber, from the Canadian Warplane Heritage Museum

RCAF Arctic Mission

While the Canadian public considered the function of Canada's military to be centred on peacekeeping, the role of the RCAF was played out in the Canadian Arctic for a very select audience. During Operation Muskox, the RCAF's responsibility went beyond supplying and guiding the ground personnel. The air force was testing new technology and generating detailed geographic and meteorological maps, often in areas never before seen by southern eyes.

Immediately after the first Soviet nuclear test in 1949, Canada, the United States and Britain stepped up efforts to monitor Soviet progress and develop countermeasures.

After the experience of Operation Muskox, the Far North was no longer considered a potential battleground for ground forces, but over the North Pole was the logical route for air attacks on southern targets and a significant route for any Strategic Air Command missions targeting the Soviet Union's heartland.

NORAD's monitoring headquarters were deep inside a Colorado mountain, with a backup location in North Bay, Ontario. Despite impressive fortification, any defensive response, whether by air or sea, required constant accurate weather information from the Arctic region. Further nuclear testing by the Soviets had to be closely monitored as well. This activity became a major responsibility of the RCAF.

Spies In The Sky

Three RCAF squadrons, the 408th, 414th, and 413th were engaged in this work, employing revamped Lancaster bombers crammed with photographic equipment, which fed data to ground stations. In 1952, 407th Squadron got on board, specifically tasked to monitor Soviet atmospheric nuclear testing. The 407's Lancasters used "scoop and filter" methods for capturing airborne particles from these tests, using a filter system developed at McGill University. The system proved to be the new standard.

The collected particles were valuable because from these particles scientists could determine the size, configuration and sophistication of the detonated devices. Between 1950 and 1962, the Soviets conducted 220 tests, and the RCAF pulled intelligence from most of them. To complement this effort, in the mid-50s the RCAF also established a secret seismic station at Flin Flon, Manitoba, as part of a worldwide "sniffer" system to detect nuclear explosions.

Through all of this defensive activity, the Soviets were not idle. Two new potential threats emerged in the Arctic during the '50s. One was the development of a long-range bomber with nuclear delivery capability about which — try as they did —Western intelligence sources could obtain no details.

The second threat was the establishment of drift stations in the Arctic. These drift stations were built on floating sheets of ice. Some of these sheets were as much as 16 kilometres miles wide and 80 kilometeres miles long, easily accommodating buildings and air strips.

The Soviets claimed these drift stations were being used purely for scientific research, but Western military intelligence suspected darker purposes. The fear was that drift stations could be used by short-range bombers to penetrate North American territory. In 1954, a time when tensions caused by the Korean War were at their height, two such drift stations were set up by the Soviets.

The RCAF, already sniffing for clues to the design and capability of the new Soviet long-range bombers, began systematic surveillance of the drift stations.

Then, in May 1958, a Lancaster flying for 408th Squadron from Alert Bay struck pay dirt, photographing a Tupolov TU-16 Badger on a drift station runway. This was not the elusive bomber, but it was a short-range cousin, which from a drift station could easily knock out Distant Early Warning Line installations, opening the way to the south.

The data from RCAF flyovers also revealed that the Soviets were setting up an early warning radar system. More recon flights were ordered. The intelligence gathered from these flights was strong enough to enable military analysts to create countermeasures to the threats.

After 1963, concurrent with the advent of satellite surveillance, the direct role of the RCAF wound down in the Arctic. On one of its last missions, the RCAF was called on to "proof" the effectiveness of the satellites.

For more than a decade, at a critical juncture in military evolution, the RCAF had a crucial role in the security of the North American continent, a silent sentinel in the shadows.

The Canadian Rangers

In August 2008, a Canadian Forces investigation team descended on a remote point of Baffin Island to investigate the report of a sub sighting. A large explosion had been observed in the area 10 days earlier. While the military was tight-lipped on its findings, it did confirm that the Canadian Rangers were factors in quickly getting the initial reports to military authorities.

In July 2009, a commercial helicopter went missing far north in Quebec. The Canadian Forces Joint Rescue Co-ordination Centre at Ontario's CFB Trenton sent in three Hercules aircraft, an Aurora patrol plane from Greenwood, Nova Scotia, and a Canadian Coast Guard helicopter to carry out the hunt. Six days of searching from the air produced no evidence.

But on Day Five of the search, Canadian Rangers, although not officially deployed, had joined the mission. A day and half later, Rangers in a small boat spotted the wreckage of the helicopter upside down in a ravine, its two occupants dead.

In both of these cases, Northern Canadian Rangers' boots on the ground proved invaluable. But for two lessons learned from Operation Muskox, the Rangers might not have been there.

MCpl Kevin Paul, Canadian Forces Combat Camera DND IS2008-3134

A Canadian Ranger from the 1st Canadian Ranger Patrol Group (1 CRPG) near Eureka, Ellesmere Island, Nunavut.

First, a large-scale land invasion moving from north to south from the Arctic was deemed virtually impossible due to climate and terrain, thus the Arctic provided a natural defence. Still, Canada needed an official presence in its Arctic territory, one with a very special character.

The cost to recruit, train, equip and base conventional military forces across the Arctic would have been astronomical, definitely a dead end in the post-World War II years of defence cost-cutting. The Canadian Rangers offered a solution.

The Frigid Front Line

In 1947, hardly a year after Operation Muskox, the Canadian Rangers were formed, based on a WW II model, the Pacific Coast Militia Rangers. In effect, the PCMRs were coast watchers posted along the British Columbia and Yukon coastlines to watch for Japanese incursions. At their peak, the PCMRs consisted of 15,000 volunteers in 138 communities.

Canadian Rangers were recruited throughout the Arctic. Most were (and still are) Inuit. They knew the subtleties and savagery of the northern land and sea. That knowledge was essential for survival on ice and barrens, the result of the experiences of generations.

In 1947, each Ranger was issued a Lee-Enfield rifle, 200 rounds of ammunition and a red arm band. The Lee Enfield has proven so dependable it is still used today. The Rangers' official duties consisted of some abbreviated annual training and specific assignments such as search and rescue, training of regular troops, and annual sovereignty patrols. The training leaned heavily toward use of radios and other location/communication devices adapted to cold weather conditions.

The Rangers were not the so-called "Saturday soldiers" reservists, often maligned by the professionals. If anything, it was the professionals who had to defer to the Rangers and climb the learning curve when they went north. Not everyone could live off this land, build an igloo, hunt seals, recognize treacherous pressure ridges or shelter in a blizzard when the temperature dropped to -50 and winds gusted across the flatlands at over 100 kilometres an hour.

Today, there are nearly 5,000 Canadian Rangers operating from 165 communities, and some of their annual sovereignty patrols have become legendary.

In 2002, a patrol of 33 Rangers trekked from Resolute Bay to the magnetic North Pole and back, 1,700 kilometres in 16 days. In 2006, five Ranger teams travelled over 5,000 kilometres in Nunavut to test equipment and identify potential locations for air fields.

Perhaps the most unusual thing about the Canadian Rangers is the respect they are given in their home communities. From their inception to the present day, they have been strong positive influences. Their inspiration is responsible for the formation of the Young Canadian Rangers, young people between 12 and 18, who in 2007 numbered 3,800.

KAPYONG: VICTORY GOES TO THE PRINCESS

Canada's military has seen action in almost every inhospitable climate and on every mean terrain on earth. Korea was one of the worst.

The legendary cold and wind at Winnipeg's Portage and Main could not compare to those on the wintry hilltops in Korea. The ground thawed to mud in the daytime and froze to rock at night. In summer, soldiers trudged through flooded rice paddies polluted with human excrement. Insufferable humidity, insect life and diseases could be as lethal as any weapon.

Troops of B Company, 2nd Battalion, Princess Patricia's Canadian Light Infantry, North Korea.

On the night of April 22, 1951, a massive assault was launched against UN defenders in the Kapyong River Valley. More than 200,000 Chinese and North Korean soldiers were set to break through UN lines and capture the South Korean capital of Seoul. The UN defenders could not hold: the South Koreans, the British, the American and the Australians fell back.

The Chinese now turned their attention to Hill 677 and the Canadians.

Lt.-Col James R. Stone was in command of the Princess Patricia's Canadian Light Infantry on the hill. Stone had taken part in the invasion of Sicily in WWII and in the Italian Campaign, where he was awarded the Military Cross for single-handedly wiping out an enemy gun emplacement that had been holding up his unit's advance.

Stone had an afternoon to position his four companies to advantage. Settled in shallow slit trenches scratched from loose rock and scrub, all the soldiers could do was wait and watch, not realizing they would be facing the assault of an entire veteran division of the Chinese army.

The Chinese waited until night and attacked in waves. Blowing whistles and bugles, hurling grenades, most of them armed with automatic weapons – so-called burp guns – they surged over the Canadian positions.

Despite suffering significant casualties, the stubborn Pats repeatedly beat them back, at times fighting hand-to-hand in the dark. At one point, the Canadians called down artillery fire on their own positions to halt a Chinese rush. Taking cover in their slit trenches, they waited out a barrage that exploded at tree-top level and scoured the ground above them.

In the morning, the Pats still held Hill 677, but they were now surrounded by Chinese. Precision airdrops of supplies to the hilltop gave the Pats what they needed to hang on. They stalled the Chinese offensive long enough for other UN forces to reinforce positions and prevent the Chinese from reaching Seoul.

For their work that night, the 2nd Battalion, Princess Patricia's Canadian Light Infantry was awarded Presidential Unit Citations, one from the United States and one from the Republic of Korea, an honour unique to this day for a Canadian unit.

DOCTOR ON CALL – THE GREAT IMPOSTER

Finding doctors to serve in the Canadian Forces was never been easy, A doctor signing up for Korea was a particularly rare occurrence.

When one enlistee walked into a New Brunswick Royal Canadian Navy recruiting office in March 1951, he wasn't just fast-tracked through the induction process; he was rocketed through in three days (instead of the normal 8 unwarranted 10 weeks). His name was Dr. Joseph Cyr. So he said, and so his credentials confirmed.

The Royal Canadian Navy had actually enlisted Ferdinand Demara, a man later to become known as the Great Impostor. Before becoming a "doctor," Demara had worked professionally in education, psychology, and zoology, though he was unqualified in all these fields. And the closest he'd come to being a medical man was in briefly holding a position as a hospital orderly.

A Quick Study

In June that year, the new "Dr. Cyr" was aboard *HMCS Cayuga*, a destroyer bound for Korea. He'd had no time to bone up on medical matters, but he got lucky in being assigned a knowledgeable assistant.

He was subjected to a trial by fire almost immediately. The captain of the *Cayuga* happened to be in agony because of a bad tooth. And he expected his ship's doctor to serve as a dentist.

Demara had been reading every medical text and reference book he could find in the sick bay. The best he could dig up on the subject of dentistry was a skimpy handbook.

He injected a magnificent dose of novocaine into the captain's jaw and, fastening his pliers on the offending tooth, he pushed, pulled, wiggled and twisted until the tooth came out — no breaks, no chips, no torn gums. From that point on, he had the captain's confidence.

The destroyer was ordered into action along the Korean coast, and that meant treating the wounded. Demara did remarkably well, setting broken bones, extracting bullets and shrapnel fragments.

Too Good to Last

Demara owes his ultimate undoing to the success of "Dr. Cyr." Early in September, the Cayuga took aboard three severely wounded men who had failed to respond to initial treatment. Realizing the gravity of their wounds, Demara chose to operate on them before they were moved from the Cayuga's deck, treating them simultaneously. The worst was a gaping chest wound. The "doctor" collapsed a lung, extracted a bullet, cleaned the wound and saved the man's life. In fact, he saved all three men.

A Royal Canadian Navy public relations officer saw a great story. When he suggested it to "Dr. Cyr," the good doctor hesitated. Then, later, inexplicably, he agreed. The story received fine coverage in New Brunswick through the Canadian Press wire service.

Unfortunately for Demara, one of the readers was the real Dr. Joseph Cyr, who eventually called the RCMP. In due course, the Great Impostor was undone.

After navigating some stormy seas over the matter, the Royal Canadian Navy quietly gave Fred Demara an honourable discharge as well as his back pay, active service bonus and other benefits. He was a fraud and an embarrassment, to be sure, but the men he saved no doubt saw him as something of a hero.

Why Demara engaged in his masquerade is anybody's guess. Perhaps he was simply a brilliant mimic with a short attention span for ordinary life. When asked to describe his motives, Demara is said to have responded: "Rascality, pure rascality."

SOMALIA: MISSION IMPOSSIBLE

In Somalia during the first half of 1993, Canadian Forces faced the toughest peacekeeping assignment in their post-Cold War history.

For years, civilians in large parts of Somalia had been victimized by famine. Violent criminal warlords used food as leverage to secure or expand their control. These warlords had no conscience when it came to allowing thousands of their fellow Somalis, including children, to die.

Peacekeepers in Somalia.

Somalia had no working governmental authority. In Mogadishu, the country's largest port city, an estimated 20,000 heavily armed bandits prowled the streets night and day. About a fifth of them were sponsored by rival warlords. They fought and killed for two commodities — the food and medical supplies shipped into the country by the United Nations and foreign aid agencies. The aid was meant for people in the countryside, who were suffering the most. Most of it never made it outside of Mogadishu, often being hijacked while still on the docks.

Near the end of 1992, the UN had only 50 unarmed observers in Somalia. Then, in December of that year, Canada committed 900 troops to the American-led Unified Task Force I. They were tasked with bringing enough stability to the country to ensure the secure delivery and distribution of humanitarian aid.

The Canadian Airborne Regiment was assigned to secure a 30,000-square-kilometre region. Their first task was to stabilize airfields, the plan being to bypass Mogadishu and fly aid supplies directly to the stricken areas.

The rural airfields were in serious disrepair when the Canadians arrived, and the safe landing of planes was further complicated by ground fire, sometimes even ground-to-air missiles, from bandits.

As the airfields were slowly repaired and secured, supplies began to trickle into the region. Naturally, the supply trail attracted more and more Mogadishu-based bandits to the countryside, and the tension and danger increased. The Canadians continually faced sniper fire and civil unrest at the drop-off points.

Bandits were not the only challenge facing the peacekeepers in Somalia. Day after day, the troops laboured in 35 to 45 degree temperatures and humidity that ranged from 60 to 80 per cent. A constant wind churned fine gritty dust into the air, making cleanliness impossible; eating a meal without swallowing a coating of sand was a rare feat.

As to meals, cooks were not assigned to the Somalia mission, leaving peacekeepers to eat only pre-packaged rations for the duration. The local water was potentially toxic, even after boiling. Harsh living conditions and poor hygiene produced a breeding ground for a variety of lethal diseases, including cholera, typhoid, hepatitis, malaria – a buffet of tropical killers. Common, too, were parasites, scorpions and poisonous snakes.

Despite this punishing environment, the Canadian peacekeepers, sometimes teaming up with development workers, were able to build roads and bridges and repair buildings in many of the villages. They were the first to re-establish schools and recruit teachers. In Mogadishu, sailors from HMCS Preserver volunteered time and skills to restore an orphanage. Much of this work was outside their central military role.

These efforts did not go unacknowledged by many Somalis. The Canadian departure from the country in June 1993 was seen as a misfortune. They had provided security, not only with their armed presence but by "leading from behind," successfully encouraging and assisting local people to begin putting the fabric of their society back together.

The Somalia Affair

Despite the good they did, the Canadian Forces contingency left Somalia under a very dark cloud. Over the next few months came revelations of a critical breakdown of discipline and leadership among Canadian soldiers in Somalia. Incidents of murder, torture, hazing activities and a subsequent cover-up by military brass all came to light.

Now the same media frenzy that had built up public pressure to send the Canadian Forces into this short-term Mission Impossible set its sights on blackening the entire peacekeeping mission. The new Liberal government's reaction was to disband the Canadian Airborne Regiment and call a commission of inquiry.

To some military leaders and citizens, the sweeping knee-jerk response to the affair was overkill. They saw the elite Canadian Airborne Regiment dissolved and its surviving members scattered into other units of the Forces almost overnight. Though there had certainly been wrongdoing for which severe penalties should have been paid, the cleanup only served to spread the stain.

Because of the actions of a relatively small group of people, and the shame of the subsequent cover-up, the image of the Canadian Forces, with its proud history and exemplary role in modern peacekeeping efforts, was irrevocably tarnished.

THE HEART OF DARKNESS

The Rwandan genocide that occurred during the summer of 1994, carried out largely over the space of 100 days saw the systemic slaughter of between 800,000 and one million people. Hundreds of thousands more were displaced to makeshift refugee camps outside the Rwandan border. The conflict continues to this day.

Rwanda in 1993 was overpopulated and desperately impoverished. Most arable land had been leeched of nutrients years earlier, and feeding the population from its own resources was not possible. Two tribes dominated the country: the Hutu and the Tutsi. Tribal dominance had been shifting back and forth during the colonial reign of Belgium, and at this time, the numbers were sitting at about 85 per cent Hutu and 15 per cent Tutsi.

Lieutenant General Roméo Dallaire in Rwanda

Decades of subjugation had boiled over in 1959 into a ferocious civil war. The wanton slaughter of Tutsi civilians caused the flight of tens of thousands to refugee camps in neighbouring countries. It was the Tutsi sons and daughters of these refugees who determined to get revenge and win back a place for themselves in Rwanda.

Despite arms and military advisers supplied by France, the Hutu government was hard-pressed. The UN attempted to intervene with an arms embargo, but weapons continued to find a way to both sides. Finally the government and rebels were lured to the bargaining table and an agreement was negotiated that provided the rebels with a narrow strip of Rwandan territory.

By late 1993, Canadian Forces in Rwanda were spread thin, having at times to draw heavily on their reservists to maintain troop strength. They already had a substantial presence in a dozen or more other countries on behalf of the UN or NATO when they were called upon to increase their interest in Rwanda.

Canadian Lt.-Gen. Romeo Dallaire, a veteran officer with many years of NATO experience, was given command of his first peacekeeping assignment in Rwanda. As it turned out, he was thrust unprepared into Africa's heart of darkness, and by all accounts, abandoned.

Enter Dallaire

Soon after his arrival, Dallaire was reporting to his UN bosses in New York the gory details of violent conflicts between rebel and government forces. He catalogued what appeared to be selective assassinations and random multiple murders. The government in Rwanda blamed these incidents on the rebels and vice versa.

In February, Dallaire's intelligence told of a substantial faction within the government and military that appeared bent on the persecution of Tutsis. This was perpetrated under the guise of bringing rebel infiltrators to task. Intelligence reported widespread distribution of free radios across the country and of blatant hate broadcasts from government-controlled radio stations encouraging violence against Tutsis. At the same time, rebel forces were becoming more active.

Dallaire requested more troops and permission to undertake proactive intervention to get the jump on these looming issues. He felt that a strong, no-nonsense UN military presence was essential. His requests were denied, and subsequent requests were unanswered. The UN and its most influential member countries, including the United States, didn't see the sense in an intervention that would be expensive and cost lives.

Dallaire and his tiny force were left to "keep the peace" in a country where there was no peace to keep.

The Answer Was No

On April 6, 1994, Rwandan President Juvenal Habyarimana, a Hutu moderate trying to hold the country together, was killed in a plane crash, probably an assassination ordered by anti-Tutsi hardliners in the government. By nightfall on April 7, most of the moderates in the government and their families were either killed

Lieutenant General Roméo Dallaire

by death squads going from house to house or had managed to find safe refuge. Many of these people were also Hutu.

Among the dead was the country's Prime Minister Agathe Uwilingiyimana and her husband. Shortly after the news, Dallaire was shown the mutilated bodies of 10 Belgian paratroopers captured earlier by "dissident" government troops.

Blaming the Tutsi rebels for the death of the prime minister, government radio began calling for all Hutus to rise up and carry out a wholesale elimination of the Tutsis in Rwanda, going so far as to read death lists for communities across the country. The genocide began in earnest, led by bands that had clearly been instructed ahead of time. The rebels, meanwhile, launched a major assault that began beating back government troops. It was only a matter of time before they would capture Kigali, the nation's capital.

Dallaire was powerless. He could order his forces to act but, being outnumbered and under-armed, they would have been overpowered very quickly. He continued to plead for UN reinforcement to no avail.

The rules of engagement were amended, at least: though his forces were still prohibited from intervening in what the UN characterized as an internal matter, they were permitted to use deadly force if their lives were threatened. Finally, Dallaire could use his resources to defend the safety of non-residents, diplomatic corps, and his soldiers.

A few weeks after the genocide began, a journalist reported on a 12-year old boy at a roadblock carrying a machete dripping blood and wearing a pale blue UN beret. On his face there was a menacing grin, and in his eyes, nothing. The daily fatalities exceeded even what the Nazis had achieved in the death camps of WWII. Dallaire and his peacekeepers witnessed all of it.

Return To Canada

Dallaire returned to Canada in September 1994. Post-traumatic stress took a cruel toll on his health. Adding to his grief, some critics blamed him, as the peacekeeping force commander, for promising safety when he knew he could not provide it. Dallaire left the Canadian Forces, and slowly recovered.

He is now a Canadian senator and works on international issues, most notably genocide prevention and elimination of the use of child soldiers.

DEALING WITH DISASTER

Late in the afternoon of January 12, 2010, Haiti was shattered by an earthquake that registered 7 on the Richter scale.

By nightfall on January 12 the air space over the Port-au-Prince airport was stacked with planes bringing relief supplies to the earthquake-devastated Haitian people. A plane would periodically drop from the throng and make a delicate instrument landing on the battered runway. Near dawn, one of these was a Canadian Forces plane carrying a specialized Canadian Forces team.

The damage was catastrophic. Haiti needed everything — search and rescue teams, water, food, medical support, security. By the 13th, Canadian Forces had four of its C-17 heavy transport planes flying relief supplies in and airlifting Canadian survivors out. Two navy ships, the frigate *HMCS Halifax* and the destroyer *HMCS Athabaskan*, were also en route.

Also en route was the Canadian Forces Disaster Assistance Response Team (DART), already recognized as among the most expert and experienced at providing early disaster assistance anywhere in the world.

Avoiding the supply log-jam in Port-au-Prince, the DART base was established at the smaller port city of Jacmel. DART engineers successfully got the Jacmel seaport and airport back in operation. The latter, Haiti's second largest, was soon receiving as many as 180 flights daily, guided in and out by Canadian Forces on the ground.

By the end of January, DART was purifying 26,000 litres of water daily for Jacmel survivors. Its medical staff was treating 300 patients daily, stretching its planned capacity by 50 or more. By then, other Canadian Forces personnel were able to clear enough roads for DART to send mobile medical teams into areas that had received no help since the earthquake.

Best In The World

Canadians didn't know much about DART before the Haiti earthquake as they are not considered peacekeepers and do not work in war zones. Yet, having the lowest fixed budget in the Canadian Forces hasn't stopped them from doing Canada proud.

DART is a quick response unit made up of four specialized units: medical, engineering, security and logistics. They are not first-responders when disasters strike but they come in hard on their heels when asked by the host country.

Given the nature of its missions, the DART unit has thankfully never had an assignment in Canada. We have had no catastrophic hurricanes, no tsunamis washing thousands of people into the sea, nor horrendous earthquakes crumbling our cities.

The Canadian government and Canadian Forces were spurred to form DART after witnessing the horrors of the Rwanda genocide and the living conditions faced by tens of thousands of refugees resulting from the genocide. Since then, the unit has successfully undertaken emergency missions in Turkey, Pakistan, Sri Lanka, and Honduras.

While the medical unit is not equipped to perform surgeries, it can provide diagnoses, including X-rays and laboratory services, along with pharmaceuticals, immediate first aid, inoculations, obstetrics and a variety of early preventive measures. It has the capacity to diagnose and treat as many as 250 patients daily.

Just as important, the team's mere presence provides a psychological boost to victims, the confidence that help is available in the face of what is incomprehensible and traumatic destruction.

Water

In most areas hit by a massive natural disaster, access to potable water can mean the difference between life and death. In 1999 in Turkey, following an earthquake, DART purified 2.5 million litres of water and monitored some 50 local water sources to ensure their safety.

A year earlier, the unit was in Honduras after a hurricane. Helicopters from CFB Petawawa had to fly the team into the devastated area. In less than two months, they produced safe water and chlorinated wells sufficient for 15,000 isolated people.

Following the 2004 tsunami in southeast Asia, DART treated more than 7,500 patients, provided 3.5 million litres of water and rescued 70,000 people trapped by floods. Its engineering section repaired roads, bridges and schools. In Turkey they erected tent shelters for 2,500 homeless survivors.

Relatively unheralded once again in late 2005, after an earthquake in Pakistan, DART quickly provided medical care to nearly 12,000 people and purified 3.8 million litres of water. They arrived in Pakistan in late October and had finished their work by December 4, handing off mopping-up efforts to Pakistani authorities and international aid organizations.

No other country in the world has a team quite like the stand-by DART unit. Although it operates out of CFB Trenton, its specialists are on active duty across the country, assembling at Trenton only when the call goes out to them.

HUMANITARIAN RELIEF
AND THE CANADIAN FORCES

Around the world Canadian Forces have been involved in peacekeeping, training, security and police actions. There is another role that can be even more important: providing humanitarian relief. Below is a list of just 20 of these humanitarian missions.

1956:	Greece, earthquake relief
1960:	Chile, earthquake relief
1960:	Congo, famine
1960:	Morocco, earthquake relief
1962:	Iran, earthquake relief
1968:	famine relief (where)
1970:	Peru, earthquake relief
1972:	Nicaragua, earthquake relief
1973:	West Africa, famine relief
1980:	Algeria, earthquake relief
1985:	Mexico City, earthquake relief
1988:	Ethiopia, famine relief
1992:	Florida, response to Hurricane Andrew
1993:	Sudan, famine relief
1992-1996:	Former Yugoslavia, humanitarian aid
2005:	New Orleans, response to Hurricane Katrina
2005:	Sri Lanka, tsunami relief
2005:	Pakistan, earthquake relief
2008:	New Orleans, response to Hurricane Gustav
2010:	Haiti, earthquake relief

Source: Department of National Defence.

MEDICINE AND THE MILITARY

Military action, so often synonymous with death and carnage, is also an engine that drives rapid advances in medical science, personal safety and general health.

Immediate front-line treatment and rapid evacuation methods were developed by military forces in the field and have since become keystones in rapid-response disaster relief work. The same applies to triage, the immediate classification of wounds by severity, conceived on the battlefields and now commonplace in emergency wards and trauma centres throughout the world.

Medical personnel carry a casualty to field hospital, Bosnia.

DND ISC94-5012A-04

Mobile medical facilities, not just ambulances but hospitals with surgical capabilities, are another common medical tool that was conceived in battle. In fact, Canadian Forces relief efforts in Haiti included shipping in an entire field hospital, held in reserve since its previous use during the Gulf War.

As a result of these innovations, the proportion of fatalities among wounded has dropped dramatically since the Crimean War. During the Crimean War and World War I, wounded had to be hauled from the lines in horse-drawn ambulance wagons, sometimes for long distances whilst under fire, just to reach forward aid stations. Infection, disease, and poor diet were as deadly as rifles and artillery on both sides of conflicts.

In Afghanistan today, helicopters carrying trained medical personnel can evacuate wounded men and women with remarkable speed, critical to saving lives and limbs.

The coalition forces hospital at Kandahar is a fully equipped trauma facility, swinging into action less than 30 minutes after the helicopters get the first call. Along with an acute care ward and three operating theatres, the hospital has a CT scanner, invaluable for fast identification of catastrophic injuries. A neurosurgeon and other specialists are on call to treat soldiers and civilians alike, approximately two-thirds of whom have been injured by improvised explosive devices(IEDs).

Quick access to treatment facilities is not the only arrow in the military medical quiver. In the field, new materials have been put to use, including more effective tourniquets and quick-clotting bandages. These are sure to find their way into the standard supply racks inside civilian ambulances and other first-responder vehicles.

Canadian Forces medics are now receiving more and better training through the Canadian Forces Medical/Dental School. The Canadian military has worked steadily to improve medical services and facilities for its personnel. This dedicated effort included the opening in 2009 of a new 80,000 square-foot, $23-million Health Services Centre in Ottawa.

Along with improvements in treatment, the Canadian Forces also place a high value on the prevention of injuries. Adjacent to CFB Valcartier is the Defence and Research Development Centre, which works on everything from improving body armour to vehicle blast protection, primarily with the objective of reducing the number and severity of injuries.

DANGEROUS FOOTING

By the end of 1995, Afghanistan had been seeded with 10 million landmines, and few people knew where they were.

Two things that are known is that more Canadians have been killed or wounded by IEDs in Afghanistan than by bullets and bombs, and that there would be a

Capt. Bill Harding teaches Afghan refugees how to recognize and disarm mines found in Afghanistan.

lot more if not for the skill and cool nerves of the Canadian military engineers and ordnance personnel who seek for, and disarm, them.

The Taliban do not need rocket scientists or a well-tooled factory to make IEDs; assembly instructions can be found on the Internet. Training manuals on how to disarm them can be turned around for use as guides to building them. Added to that, hundreds of Afghans were trained during the '90s to disarm mines. It isn't a stretch to assume some of these were Taliban, and if they know how to disarm them, they know how to construct them.

As for materials, these are readily available. The IED that killed four Canadian soldiers and a journalist in Kandahar province on December 30, 2009, was determined to be an HME (homemade explosive). It was planted in a tunnel under a road, a technique used effectively by the Sicilian Mafia during the '90s.

IEDs come in all sizes and configurations. Some would be aptly called booby-traps, detonated by pressure (or release of pressure), trip wires or movement. These normally strike individual soldiers. Larger IEDs, buried in roadways and trails, are powerful enough to destroy armoured vehicles and can be detonated remotely, sometimes by cellphone.

Canadian Forces have been responding to the IED threat in many ways. Before deployment in Afghanistan, all Canadian ground forces receive specialized training in how to identify and locate potential IEDs.

IEDs can be identified with metal detectors. But this method cannot distinguish between a device and scattered scrap metal left from decades of warfare, or IEDs constructed without metal. Another downside is that using metal detectors can slow down convoys, inviting ambushes.

Another tool is the use of explosive-sniffing dogs. The Canadian Forces deploy about 30 dogs for this work. And the effectiveness of the dogs can be limited by terrain, climate, and the periodic need for lengthy retraining. Dogs have been especially useful in detecting explosives inside buildings and vehicles.

Also available to engineers is the U.S.-developed handheld standoff mine detection system, initially used for landmine clearance but now available for limited use to locate IEDs. In 2010, the detection arsenal took another stride when air surveillance for suspicious activity was added.

Engineers check village elders before meeting with neighbouring village leaders, Somalia.

DND ISC93-10184

Mine Warfare

A farmer sowing rice in a remote Vietnam paddy has his legs suddenly blown off and bleeds to death in the mud, killed by a 40-year-old landmine.

Another farmer with perfectly arable land in Somalia abandons his farm. He takes with him his whole family and all the belongings they can carry on their backs, joining thousands of other people wasting away in refugee camps. His fields have been sown with mines. So have those of his neighbours.

A six-year-old child in Bosnia discovers what appears to be a delightful plastic toy. When it explodes, the child loses an arm and is permanently blinded. Not all landmines are metal.

After years of living in an overcrowded, disease-ridden Pakistan refugee camp, an Afghan who fled the Russia-Afghanistan battlegrounds is allowed to return to his home village. Trudging hopefully along an isolated mountain footpath, the refugee is blown to pieces by a leftover mine, his fate determined by a single step.

Wherever in the world there is armed military conflict, mines have become almost as ubiquitous as bullets. They wait with deadly purpose for the unwary tread of a soldier's boot, and when the battles are over, they remain in place, often to kill or maim innocent civilians.

Throughout the Cold War, members of the Canadian Military Engineers had focused on the probability of mine warfare; after all, explosive mines of one form or another had been around since the Chinese invented them in the 13th century. Even Leonardo Da Vinci tried his hand at designing them. Man's ingenuity generally peaks during times of war, and with each war, mines were improved. Militarily speaking, they were cheap and effective.

Mines initially were weapons of formal armies, who documented their locations. The placement of mines eventually became disorganized throughout times of civil conflict and blanket dispersal, dropped by helicopters over vast areas of Vietnam, for example.

When conflicts abated, the resettlement of mined areas brought the horror to life for civilians. As late as 1960, mines sown by Confederate soldiers during the Civil War were discovered near Savannah, Georgia. They were still live.

Canadians Play Their Part

Canadians were part of an initiative begun in 1989 to provide "humanitarian de-mining" assistance. This mission brought Canadian Military Engineers into Pakistan, Afghanistan, Bosnia-Herzegovina. Kuwait, Iraq, Croatia, Somalia, East Timor, Kosovo, Ethiopia, Macedonia, Eritrea, Angola and Mozambique.

Canadian Forces expertise was a fortuitous resource for the UN when it resolved to begin de-mining the world. In many countries, Canada quickly took a lead role. Not only were Canadian troops risking their lives in the field, but they also were training local citizens and members of aid organizations to help carry out the work.

Success was limited, partly because of cost, partly because the work is time-consuming and partly because civil infrastructures were unworkable, as could be expected in nations coming out of profoundly destructive civil conflict. Nevertheless, a significant aspect of Canadian peacekeeping since 1989 has been humanitarian de-mining.

MOST HEAVILY MINED COUNTRIES

Country	Number of land-mines per square mile	Estimated total number of land-mines
Bosnia and Herzegovina	152	3,000,000
Cambodia	143	10,000,000
Croatia	137	3,000,000
Egypt	60	23,000,000
Iraq	59	10,000,000
Afghanistan	40	10,000,000
Angola	31	15,000,000
Iran	25	16,000,000
Rwanda	25	250,000

Source: United Nations Department of Humanitarian Affairs.

Note: There is too little information about some countries. such as VietNam, to include them in the estimates.

Modern Mine Detection

The scope of the problem faced by Canadian engineers and those of other nations remains immense. In Angola, for example, 15 million live mines are still in the ground, although the country's population is only 10 million. In Mozambique, one of the poorest nations on earth, wells can not be approached for water, fishing boats cannot be launched from shores, farm fields can't be sown or cultivated because an estimated 500,000 mines are still in the ground.

One of the strategies recently introduced in Mozambique is the Gambian pouched rat. The rat is cheaper and more accurate than metal detectors, and its weight, about three kilograms, is light enough to prevent detonation if a mine is stepped on. The rat is easier to train than a dog, and the training sticks longer.

The rats are trained to associate the smell of explosives with that of food. On long leashes, they can cover far more ground in a day than a human with a metal detector. Rats are also native to Mozambique. Formerly a scourge, they are now lifesavers.

In Sri Lanka, mongooses are being attached to a simple remote-controlled robot. The added element of the robot enables the operator to direct the mongoose and remain safe at the same time. As with the pouch rat, mongooses are trained to respond to the smell of explosives.

In Israel, experiments are underway to use pigs to sniff out mines. Again the association of explosives and food is the incentive. Research indicates that the pigs can be trained in half the time it takes to train a dog and stay much more focused while on the job, probably because eating is their primary interest.

One experimental approach underway to locate suspected minefields is to blanket an area with a bacteria that fluoresces when it comes into contact with vapours from explosives. Bees are also being studied as a potential means to identify the presence of explosives over broad areas.

The theory is that bees can be conditioned to associate explosives with food, then be tracked as they go about searching for pollen. Upon their return to their hives, the dust sticking to them can be analyzed for trace explosive components that have leached into the soil and made their way up the food chain into vegetation.

THE BAND IN THE BACK

In every branch of the Canadian Forces, an uninterrupted supply chain is critical, and that's where the band of almost invisible military personnel in the back does its work.

A requisition for a basic item such as a new pair of boots passes through many hands before those boots reach the soldier, and the boots themselves may travel thousands of kilometres before they're laced onto his or her feet.

The process involves not only the clerk who generates the requisition but also those who ensure the boots move along the supply chain; the stores gopher who pulls them from a shelf; the stores clerk who makes sure they're in a planeload of supplies for Kandahar; the forklift operator who unloads the plane; the stores receiver; and the supply dispenser.

At any given time there may be 500 pairs of combat boots warehoused at Kandahar or other supply depots; these have arrived along the same supply chain. And let's not forget the accounting clerk who cuts the cheque to pay for the boots or the officer who OKs every requisition and cheque.

Canadian ground forces depend almost as much on their vehicles as on their boots. Dealership warranties and service are of little use in a rugged combat zone like Afghanistan; an untimely breakdown here can be fatal. The vehicles are kept running from behind the scenes by skilled, usually creative mechanics, machinists, and welders. When parts are unavailable, repairs may have to be jury-rigged or fabricated. A coveted skill is the ability to cannibalize bits and pieces of junked vehicles in order to keep others running.

Another key group operating behind the scenes keeps the planes and helicopters flying, not so easy when sensitive parts are subject to constant corrosive dust, scorching heat and high humidity. To do this requires not just a knowledge of the aircraft's mechanics, but also knowledge that comes from years of training and experience.

And let's not forget this is a shooting war. The weapons specialists also have a vital role. Their work goes beyond their role in dispensing bombs, rockets, artillery shells and bullets. Other than personal weapons, which are individual responsibilities, armourers are responsible for weapons as diverse as heavy machine-guns and mortars; vehicular weapons systems like tanks and heavy artillery; a variety of explosive devices, and likely many more the general public doesn't know exist.

On The Water

Rarely visible are the below-decks sailors in the Canadian navy. They work in the engine rooms, communications section and galley, among other places in the bowels of the ships. Frigates crammed with state of the art electronics often have some bona fide computer geeks in their crew who are super-skilled at optimizing the electronics' capabilities.

Canada's able seamen are able indeed. The sailor scrubbing pots in the galley may at a moment's notice be tasked with calibrating depth charges. The steward who serves in the officers' mess may also be part of the ship's damage-control team. A supply clerk may become part of a boarding party conducting searches for drugs, illegal immigrants, pirates, or embargoed goods.

The Canadian Forces have always been lean, even during World War II. Concerning resources other than human, repair has always taken precedence over replace. Theirs is not and cannot be a throw-away culture. Functioning this way takes special skills that frequently go unnoticed. Sometimes duct tape does the job, but most times long training, dedication and creativity work better.

As most behind-the-scenes military personnel see it, they're just doing their jobs. Yet their jobs are essential. Some may seem menial and many may seem dull, but they go a long way toward helping bring the men and women "outside the wire" back inside safely. For that recognition, perhaps it's a blessing that journalists have finally discovered them.

A SILENT REQUIEM: "HERE THEY COME"

Outside of friends, family members and grateful citizens in the many countries where they sacrificed their lives, Canada's fallen soldiers and their contributions remain almost invisible — symbolic certainly, but not integral to the here and now of daily life in Canada, the country they served and for which they gave their lives. In one part of Canada, this picture has dramatically changed.

Today, these heroes are no longer buried in the faraway countries where they fell. Today, they are coming home. Their journeys begin in Afghanistan in flag-draped caskets. Shortly after their plane lands at CFB Trenton, a solemn repatriation service is conducted with family and fellow soldiers.

Often the landing is broadcast nationwide on television. Then in a convoy of up to 20 vehicles, their bodies are driven along the Macdonald-Cartier Freeway, or Highway 401, to Toronto.

Since the first convoy in 2002, every time a soldier's body is repatriated a spontaneous phenomenon occurs along the 172-kilometre route.

Canadians from all walks of life gather on every overpass and line the shoulders of the highway. The weather doesn't matter; the time of day doesn't matter. What matters is the community fellowship, the desire to recognize and pay tribute to fallen fellow Canadians.

Some people are at the same places every time; others are first-timers. Those who have come once often come back again. Some have travelled long distances; others may have left their offices, shops or factories in the local areas. There are veterans in familiar blazers and berets, workers in hard hats, parents with toddlers in tow.

Eventually, a murmur runs through the gathering: "Here they come." A long way off, the convoy appears, escorted front and back by local police and fire vehicles, lights flashing. Inside the convoy are the hearse(s), more cars carrying family members and military vehicles carrying a Canadian Forces honour escort.

As the convoy passes along the route, Canadians flags and banners rise along the highway and on the overpasses, too many to count. The people wave to demonstrate respect, support and reassurance, in effect, to strengthen the bond between Canadians, their protectors, and the families of their protectors.

In 2007, Ontario's Ministry of Transport officially named that section of highway the Highway of Heroes.

Chapter · VI:
Welcome Home
Canada's Veterans

For most of us, November 11 is a day to pause and consider, a day to silently recall the sacrifices of yesterday and today and to ponder those that are sure to come.

For those who have served, these memories do not come only on Remembrance Day. They are a permanent fixture of life and do not fade.

Some of these memories satisfy, as a job well done can do. Others are painful and disturbing. For veterans, sharing them outside the military community can be extremely difficult; they are too far beyond the experience of their civilian peers, oftentimes they cannot even be shared with the veterans' families.

The difficulties in adjusting to civilian life after military service have been long recognized. First Nations veterans, for example, came home from both world wars to find they still could not vote in Canadian elections unless they gave up all treaty rights.

The special circumstances of Hong Kong survivors were ignored by succes- . sive federal governments, seemingly more bent on denying them benefits than acknowledging their sacrifice. Canada's merchant mariners, the key to supplying the Allied war effort in World War II, were denied all benefits.

Aware of these and other inequities, veterans eventually realized they would have to bring about change on their own. In 1926, veterans established what is now known as the Royal Canadian Legion. Together with The War Amps, founded in 1920, the Navy League, the Corp of Commissionaires and others, the legion provided transitional and ongoing support and services such as counselling and job placement. The legion and partners also petitioned for improved veterans' benefits such as retraining and medical services.

These organizations have long argued that it is not enough to infuse military culture and to train men and women to go into harm's way; it is also essential for Canada to assist in their return to civilian life.

Veteran's organizations and their members also make a considerable contribution to the country. Legion branches, with 360,000 members across the country regularly contribute to local charities. And for several years, The War Amps has provided prosthetics to children as a part of its mission.

These organizations are no longer alone. Canada's involvement in Afghanistan has awakened broader public awareness of the dedication and sacrifice of the Canadian Forces. Pertaining to the Forces, three new Rs have entered the Canadian lexicon: recognition, regard and respect.

AH, THE GOOD LIFE

Many Canadians still think a career in the Armed Forces is a sweet deal for anyone who wants a comfortable, guaranteed, cradle-to-grave life provided on the taxpayer's tab. It's not.

At a glance, the military seems to offer an easy solution to many career questions, laying a clear path from youth to retirement.

A recruit can reasonably expect the following scenario:

- joining cadets as a youngster
- joining the reserves later
- possibly enjoying a free university education
- enlistment in the regular forces
- retiring with a pension while still young enough to enjoy it

Along the way, the military provides housing, clothing, food and a salary. There is also a full range of medical benefits and, of course, opportunities to travel and see the world.

The public would be in error in taking this at face value or thinking these benefits do not come at a heavy price. Members of the reserves, for one, are subject to being called up at any time, whether to assist with domestic disaster relief or to be deployed into conflict zones. Many of the troops currently in Afghanistan are reservists. Those "free" university degrees aren't so free either. Their cost is paid back with years of active service in the regular forces.

That pension only kicks in after 20 years of service. That criterion covers about 30 per cent of veterans. Nearly the same percentage (28) of Canadians queried in a recent poll thought all veterans got pensions. To make ends meet, the majority of Canadian veterans must find full-time work after retirement.

The idea of travelling and seeing the world has an enticing ring to it. Unfortunately, the parts of the world many in the service get to see are the worst hellholes Mother Earth has on offer. Any natural "view" has typically been obstructed by barbed wire and blast barriers, the quaint villages are often just rubble, and the locals might be as likely to shoot a touristy soldier as barter for souvenirs.

BEYOND THE CALL

Conventional Canadian wisdom is that our old soldiers take jobs as commissionaires or spend their time chilling at the local legion and trading war stories. Maybe there is a kernel of truth to that, but it's far and away overshadowed by what they're really up to, especially in their legion halls.

Many Canadians wake up to the presence of the Royal Canadian Legion late in every October and through the first 11 days of November. That's when legion branches across the country mobilize their members to conduct their annual poppy drive, and, in Remembrance Day ceremonies, to stand proudly in the forefront as reminders of sacrifices made by Canada's military men and women and their families.

But the legion members do not sit idle for the other 11 months of the year. From 1,500 branches in Canada, the United States and Europe, members reach out to their home communities to provide support services, not only to veterans, but to citizens at large.

A good example is the Westboro Legion, Branch 480, in Ottawa. The 480 is a hub of local activities, many of which are fundraisers involving legion members and civilians alike. The branch also runs weekly bingos, and dinners, dances, teas and raffles. Its facilities are rented for private parties, community events and meetings.

The money raised by members is used for a lot more than covering the overhead costs of their building. Much of it flows directly back into the community. Here's a snapshot of where members and the branch donated their funds raised in 2009:

The Salvation Army

Ottawa Food Bank

Ottawa Mission

Ottawa Neighbourhood Services

Shepherds of Good Hope

Interval House

Dave Smith Youth Treatment Centre

Canadian Council of the Blind

Ottawa Therapy Dogs

Children's Wish Foundation

Max Keeping Foundation

Camp Banting (Canadian Diabetes Foundation)

Lions Camp Dorset

Camp Smitty

St. Brigid's Camp

Cancer Recovery Foundation (camp)

Christie Lake Kids Camp

Camp Misquah

Victims of Violence

Therapeutic Riding of Ottawa

Royal Canadian Legion Troop Morale Fund

Legion District G's Track and Field Meet

Vice-Admiral Kingsmill Cadet Corps (navy)

30th Field Artillery Cadets (army)

211 Air Cadet Squadron (air)

Veterans stand to salute the fallen ships and sailors lost during the Battle of Atlantic.

As in every legion branch, 480's members are also involved in the poppy campaign. Member projects are initiated to commemorate historic Canadian military events, and, of course, Remembrance Day ceremonies. Members' outreach activities regularly find them in local schools and at service club meetings to raise visibility and awareness.

For local veterans and their families, the 480 offers access to information on veteran services and other benefits. This has always been a key role of the Royal Canadian Legion, reaching from the ground up — local members-branch-district-provincial-national, a chain of command that has had a positive impact on government policy-making in veterans' affairs.

The volunteer person-hours donated to the 480's work are beyond counting. Multiply that commitment by the similar volunteer work of all of the branches across the country, and the contribution to the well-being of Canadian communities becomes astronomical. It doesn't leave a lot of time for trading war stories or polishing medals.

The Royal Canadian Legion has also maintained its broader advocacy role. Joining other veterans' organizations and service agencies, the legion has successfully worked to obtain equitable spousal benefits and compensation for Dieppe and Hong Kong veterans and for merchant mariners. The legion also participates in the Veterans Independence Program and Pension Review Board.

Across the country, legion members have made it their business to help cut through the bureaucratic red tape of the Veterans Affairs Department. These members were themselves veterans, many of whom served on the battlefronts, then struggled through the morass of endless forms and complex regulations separating veterans from their due. Today, these supports remain in place.

Legion branches have helped fund seniors housing and long-term care facilities, sports and cadet programs and research into diabetes and other illnesses. The interests and concerns of veterans are still the priority, the focus shifting as needs change; a case in point, dealing with post-traumatic stress disorder among veterans.

THE KEYS TO REHABILITATION

Canada is by no stretch of the imagination a welfare state in which government provides for all of a citizen's needs from cradle to grave. While government does provide some basics, many pressing social needs are met in other ways, either directly — in the form of self-help by those people affected — or by non-profit charitable organizations, which enlist the support of citizens. Historically, this has particularly been the case for Canada's military veterans.

Following the First World War, Canada's veterans formed many self-help organizations, picking up where government left off. Several of these evolved into the Royal Canadian Legion. Another, chartered in 1920, evolved into The War Amps.

World War I soldier being fitted by a prosthetist.

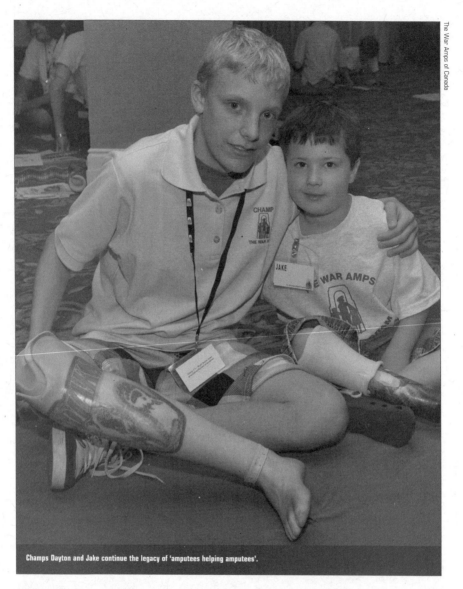

Champs Dayton and Jake continue the legacy of 'amputees helping amputees'.

Disabled war veterans had no interest in becoming burdens to their families or communities. They wanted to establish dignified, productive places in the mainstream. War Amps founder Padre Lt.-Col. Sidney Lambert marshalled these veterans and put them on the path to meet these goals, supporting one another as they went.

Lambert's mission began with a simple concept: a self-supporting sheltered workshop that provided meaningful employment plus a fair day's wage for a fair day's work.

Profits would be used to support the organization and expand its programs.

By the end of World War II, The War Amps was able to step up its services. It became a conduit for information about available rehab programs and advances in prosthetics design. Counselling, advocacy and fellowship were also available. Most important, war amputees were empowered as owners and operators of the organization.

The War Amps key tag program, begun in 1946, is well known to most adult Canadians. Perhaps not so well known are many other programs successfully fielded between then and now.

In 1953, for example, The War Amps began a program that has had far-reaching affects throughout Canada. Originally known as the Civilian Liaison Program, it extended War Amps services and expertise beyond veterans to include all amputees. Shortly after it was begun, the program was divided between adults and children in recognition that specific needs of the two groups were significantly different.

From this innovative move evolved the Child Amputee Program, or CHAMP, now providing prosthetics, counselling and education to assist children in adjusting to their amputation. In a natural progression, The War Amps began injury-prevention programs for children, including *PlaySafe*, *Safety Walk*, and *DriveSafe*.

To strengthen family support services, the *Matching Mothers Program* was begun in 1984. All of these programs are spinoffs of CHAMP. So is *JumpStart*, which provides early computer training for children with multiple amputations to help enable their independent living and full options for employment later in life.

Serving generations of Canadians in its work, The War Amps has not put aside its original mission. Remembrance of past sacrifices remains a focus, manifested in its *Military Heritage* documentaries. Taking another step beyond that, the organization initiated its *Never Again* Program in 1985, carrying its message to younger generations of Canadians.

Throughout the years, The War Amps has remained completely self-supporting, relying on donations exclusive of government funding. In itself, this is a remarkable achievement. It is also a testament that, in effect, its core members still practise what they preach.

MISTER VETERAN

Military leaders tend to have a short shelf life in the eyes of the Canadian public. Then, there's a former World War II company commander who to this day is both recognized and revered by thousands of Canadians. His name is Clifford Chadderton but many know him as Mister Veteran.

By the time Cliff Chadderton took over as chief executive officer of The War Amps in 1965, he was already recognized as a leading expert on veterans' affairs — the legislation, its implementation and its effectiveness.

When Chadderton returned from the war as an amputee, he was able to adjust and rebuild his life with the help of The War Amps. He went to work in government, rising to senior positions dealing with veterans' welfare and rehabilitation. Between 1965 and 1968, he capped this career phase as the executive director of the Woods Committee Study of veterans' pension legislation. By then, he was already busy reshaping The War Amps.

Chadderton brought vision, energy, knowledge and dedication to the organization. Today, The War Amps operates with a budget of over $18 million a year, the bulk of which is put back into programs benefiting Canadian adult and child amputees. And administrative expenses are held to less than half of what many other similar sized charities spend.

Hands On

The hands-on approach was always Chadderton's style. At age 66, he took up skiing to demonstrate to amputees that many recreational activities are not beyond reach. By then, he was already an accomplished award-winning video producer, and he turned his skiing success and the successes of other amputees, including children, into another film series.

Another wrong that needed to be righted for veterans was the CBC's much ballyhooed 1992 documentary, The Valour and The Horror. With Chadderton in the lead, the council took strong public issue with the documentary's accuracy, production values and slant. Finally, the CBC ombudsman officially discredited the film. It was found to be "seriously flawed and (it) failed to measure up to the CBC journalistic policies and broadcasting standards."

Cliff Chadderton.

As chairman of the National Council of Veteran Associations, Chadderton was often called upon to advise government and to lobby government for change as needed.

Cliff Chadderton put a deep footprint in the struggle for just veterans' benefits

Major-General Mark McQuillan (right) and Honorary Grand President of the Royal Canadian Legion, Lieutenant-General Charles Belzile, (centre) present a wreath to Major Thomas Norris to be placed at the Groesbeek Cemetery on behalf of the Royal Canadian Legion.

and for programs in support of amputees and their families. This has included the expansion of benefits for peacekeeping veterans, including disability status for post-traumatic stress disorder in the Pension Act. This achievement flies in the face of generations-old military culture and still significantly affects the lives of many veterans.

Although many War Amps programs have shifted to services to a broader community than war amputees, The association continues to regard veterans' needs as a top personal priority.

Vigorously supported by its member organizations, the national council was able to convince government to finally recognize and compensate survivors and families of World War II's tragic debacle in Hong Kong. The council also successfully went to bat for WW II's merchant mariners, who had been at the forefront of the battles of the Atlantic and St. Lawrence.

CANADA'S WALKING WOUNDED

Since 2002, psychiatric stress injuries, including post-traumatic stress disorder (PTSD),are reported to be on the rise among Canadian Forces personnel. Actually, they may not be; what may be on the rise is the frequency with which they are reported.

Shell shock was the all-inclusive term used to describe psychiatric injuries during World War I. When dealing with soldiers suffering with shell shock, psychiatrists pointed to inherent individual weaknesses that should have been identified during the sign-up and boot-camp phases of enlistment. In the field, many sufferers were disciplined as malingerers; a soldier's "stiff upper lip" was not supposed to tremble.

During World War II, the term battle exhaustion replaced shell shock. The RCAF had its own term, tending to scoff at such injuries, labelling it LMF, which stood for "low moral fibre." That condition, of course, called for discipline, perhaps demotion or even a stint in the guardhouse.

Military culture then and now dictates that true warriors never flinch. But the horror of war's violence can make the opposite inevitable, especially for military personnel who have experienced multiple deployments or involvement in protracted engagements – about one in four soldiers. They are both participants and witnesses.

In the field, soldiers suffering from such conditions may labour on. They do not want to let their comrades down and they know that even in our seemingly enlightened time, psychiatric injuries are often stigmatized. For officers, the whiff of stress injury can be a career killer. The story of the veteran who will not recount service experiences to friends or family even after decades have passed has become almost cliché.

The incidence of psychiatric stress injuries indicates that the military is beginning to come to terms with what has been a long-standing problem. It has also recognized, albeit reluctantly, that these injuries may not become obvious until years after members leave the services. Spousal abuse, marital breakdown, alcohol and drug abuse and anti-social, sometimes criminal, behaviour are seen now as possible repercussions of experiences during overseas deployments, including peacekeeping missions.

Acceptance of this condition is reflected in the increase of successful psychiatric stress disability claims since 2002. Of veterans who applied for these pensions in 2008, 60 per cent incurred their injuries a decade or more earlier. These applications, therefore, have come out of soldiers' experiences in Bosnia, Rwanda, and Somalia.

In 2002, there were 2,137 individuals receiving psychiatric disability pensions on Veteran Affairs Canada's books. Since then, as the figures below show, the numbers have risen.

Year	Number	Increase
2002	2,137	
2003	3,501	1,364
2004	4,894	1,393
200	6,491	1,597
2006	8,385	1,894
2007	10,272	1,887
2008	11,045	773
2009	11,888	843 (to October 1, 2009)

In the past, tens of thousands of Canadian soldiers with psychiatric injuries have probably been passed over. Certainly, part of this is due to the infancy of psychiatry and psychotherapy in years gone by, but much of it points to what was the prevailing military and public perception of such injuries.

Recognition of the need for support has been slow in coming, to the point that non-governmental organizations and veterans support organizations such as the legion and War Amps had to go public for change to begin to occur.

To put the situation into perspective, by the middle of 2009, about 27,000 Canadian troops had served, or were serving, in Afghanistan, not including those who served multiple stints, sometimes as many as five. Of these, about 1,000, or 3.6 per cent, sustained physical injuries. During the same period, 5.8 per cent, or nearly 1,600 troops, were diagnosed with symptoms of PTSD or depression. To be sure, some overlaps are likely, and, to be sure, the Defence Department and Veterans Affairs are now visibly on the case.

CHAPTER VII:
OUR MODERN FORCES

The breadth of operations and services undertaken by the modern Canadian Forces is generally unknown to the average citizen. Canadians are aware that our troops are very active in Afghanistan; it's hard to miss that. Many also realize that at any given time, 2,800 of our troops are in that treacherous, inhospitable theatre. But how many realize that since 2002, 32,500 military personnel have seen service there?

Canada's remarkably tiny navy (for a maritime nation) has been exceptionally busy. In November 2009, *HMCS Calgary* and *HMCS Toronto* wrapped up a six-week mission as part of Operation CARIBBE, a multinational drug interdiction effort that in 2007 and 2008, captured about 200 metric tonnes of illicit drugs annually. The surveillance capability of these ships was vital to the operation.

In early November 2009, a Canadian frigate launched and retrieved an autonomous surveillance vessel (drone), a first for our navy. This success could lead to much-enhanced monitoring of Canada's sovereignty in the Arctic.

In another day at the military office, two search and rescue specialists from the air branch parachuted onto an ice floe in Nunavut to rescue a stranded 17-year-old hunter.

In conjunction with the Ministry of Fisheries and Oceans, the Forces are actively involved in monitoring iceberg movement, which can threaten shipping lanes. As with many Canadian Forces operations, the work is carried out with other countries.

Wherever Canadian Forces operate and whatever they do, they apply a high level of technological skill, team work, equanimity and dedication. In the navy, the days of swabbing the decks and dangling in the yards to set a sail are long gone. The same applies to the air and army branches; those good old days are only memories.

The Canadian Forces are lean and sharp, ready and capable. Eventually, this phenomenal resource will come fully out of the shadows and be recognized.

LCdr Lalitha Rupesinghe surrounded by curious children at the Zainab Cobera girls school in Kabul, Afghanistan.
DND KA2004-A053D

171

DND KA2003-A158

Solider

THE BEST AND BRIGHTEST

In order to attend university, many students must put together a patchwork of student loans, bursaries, part-time and summer jobs just to scrape by for three years and earn an undergraduate degree, and complete at least four more years of this if they want a post-graduate degree. Still they have no guarantee of a job. Their only guarantee is that they'll spend the next five to 10 years paying back their loans. For many, the Canadian Forces has changed that prospect.

The Canadian Forces will cover tuition, books and fees and provide a comfortable living allowance throughout the university years, thus taking a good portion of the stress out of the academic experience.

Of course, this comes at a cost. Weekends and summers are committed to reserve officer training. In addition, upon graduation, six to eight years must be served in the regular forces. That last stipulation may seem like a lot, but perhaps not so much when balanced against the years that would be required to pay back student loans and other debt incurred while at university.

Prospective university students are aware that tuition and related costs are rising, increasing the debt they will eventually have to repay. Given all of this, maybe the Canadian Forces offer looks like a pretty good deal. In 2009, 400 students across Canada thought so.

* * *

Among the post-secondary education opportunities the Canadian Forces has on offer, the most prized remains the combined degree and Regular Officer Training Program at the Royal Military College in Kingston. Here, the serious training of Canada's future military leaders often begins.

Many of the students come from military families and/or have been cadets or spent time in the reserves, but that doesn't make them a shoo-in for admission. Annual applications exceed 1500 for the College's 300 first-year spaces. On the hunt for leadership qualities, the admissions team does meticulous work. Previous academic proficiency is scrutinized — a 70 per cent average overall is minimum, but plus-80 has become more commonplace. Value is also placed on extracurricular activities as indicators of an ability to multi-task. Past those hurdles come medical examinations, aptitude tests, and several intense, probing interviews.

With everything looking good, three weeks of rigorous boot camp ensues before first-year classes begin. ROTP training is scheduled while kids at other universities are enjoying spring break. Summer holidays are confined to a few days at best. Soldiering is 24-7 and so is training; summer's the time for field and officer training exercises.

Obviously, the Canadian Forces place a high premium on officer and specialist training, mindful that both are critical to the Forces' effectiveness, efficiency and, not least, the security of the nation. The Canadian public has set our military bar very high. The military generally strives to reach it, then sets it higher.

SUNDAY SOLDIERS

The most reliable backstop available to the regular Canadian Forces is its 27,000 reservists. Sure, sometimes they're referred to as Sunday Soldiers, but overall, they have earned remarkable respect from career military men and women at every level along the chain of command.

The reserves grew out of two Canadian military traditions — voluntarism and militias. Many of the first militia officers were former British soldiers, and it remained this way into the early 20th century.

Canada's version of a standing army and navy was modest in size by any standard, and the country's volunteer militias were often viewed by military veterans in the officer corps as something less than capable soldiers and sailors.

The Royal Military College at Kingston opened in the 1870s, providing a curriculum and discipline mirroring the British model. In 1910, Canada's Royal Canadian Navy College was established in Halifax, and by 1914, was turning out 50 graduates annually. Volunteers all, these would become the nucleus of Canada's early armed forces, a distinctly Canadian officer corps.

Unfortunately, at the outset of World War I, Canadian forces, like those of other Commonwealth countries, were often regarded as handmaids to British command, mere live bodies from the "colonies." By the end of that war, Canadian soldiers, sailors and pilots had thoroughly stripped most British commanders of that bias.

The bias would rear its ugly head again at the beginning of the Second World War, but Canadian politicians and military officers once more put paid to the billing. For the most part, Canadian forces were commanded by Canadian officers who had seats at the table when major decisions and strategies were generated. Many of these officers had come up through the ranks of Canada's reserves between wars.

Afghanistan

Fast forward to Afghanistan and Canada's 27,000 reservists and their officers, more than 75 per cent of whom are in the land forces. While there was once a time that they were part-time soldiers, those days are long gone.

Of the Princess Pats contingent that saw action during the 14-day skirmish at the Medak Pocket in Yugoslavia for example, 70 per cent were reservists. Today, up to 25 per cent of Canadian Forces members in Afghanistan are reservists. Many of them are professionals in civilian life, handling tasks for which the military would otherwise have no capability, and they do so for 20 per cent less pay than regular forces.

Reservists who volunteer for Afghanistan cease to be part-time. Their civilian lives are put on hold. Before their deployment, usually a six-to nine-month rotation, they undergo months of full-time training, bringing them up to regular force standards.

Having 65,000 regulars in the Canadian Forces may seem like a lot. So why this reliance on reservists? After all, Canada has had only about 2,800 troops in Afghanistan at any given time. But this 65,000 includes recruits in training, troops maintaining domestic bases and troops carrying out missions to satisfy other international obligations.

It also includes sailors and air force personnel providing domestic defence and aiding international enforcement efforts such as fighting drug trafficking in the Caribbean and piracy in the Indian Ocean. And many regulars are now on their third and fourth deployments to Afghanistan.

How the Canadian Forces managed to successfully carry out its Haiti earthquake and 2010 Olympic security missions simultaneously, while still maintaining obligations in other parts of the world is hard to imagine. It involves deploying 2,900 full-time reservists to the Olympics in Vancouver. Between there and Afghanistan, more than half the country's reservists were now full time, carrying out the same duties as regular forces. The military branches of Canada were scraped bare.

If the 2011 withdrawal from Afghanistan goes as planned, it will ease the Canadian Forces' manpower needs. On the other hand, rogue states, civil wars, terrorism and natural disasters could keep the pressure on, if not increase it. The relatively new, more full-time role of the reserves may not change for a long time.

WOMEN AT ARMS

In 1943, U.S. President Franklin Roosevelt officially received Ludmilla Pavlichenko at the White House. Her claim to fame: she was a sniper in the Russian Army, credited with 309 kills, 36 of whom were enemy snipers. Was this a signal to the Allies that women could successfully undertake combat roles in the modern military? If it was, Canadian commanders didn't see it until nearly 50 years later.

From the Boer War onward, the Canadian military realized the immense value of female nurses treating wounded soldiers. During World War I, Canada recruited 3,100 female nurses. Another 35,000 women were employed in Canadian munitions factories. At the time, it seems, it was acceptable for women to make the weapons but not to use them.

Not much changed during World War II. The Canadian army, navy, and air force signed up 43,000 women, and their roles were expanded. They were deemed quite capable as clerks, drivers, radio and radar operators, and, of course, as nurses – any job that did not involve combat.

In 1951, women were enlisted as part of the reserves and in 1955, they were officially integrated into the regular forces. When the branches of Canada's military were merged into the Canadian Forces, however, they were designated as "servicewomen" and remained excluded from combat.

Finally, in 1989, full integration was achieved. The issue had long ceased to be one of whether women should have combat roles. The issue was now gender equality.

The impact was noticeable by 1991. Of nearly 4,200 Canadian Forces personnel in the Gulf War theatre, 237 were women. Women would also serve in Bosnia, Rwanda, Afghanistan, and other conflict zones.

The Royal Military College went co-ed in 1979, ahead of the 1989 proclamation. Today, nearly 30 per cent of students are women.

In 2003, Lt.-Col. Jennie Carignan, serving in Afghanistan, became the first female deputy commanding officer of a combat arms unit in the Canadian military. And in 2009. command of the frigate HMCS Halifax was passed to Cmdr. Josée Kurtz, the first woman to captain a Canadian warship. Among her 220 crew members are 15 women. Kurtz is a 20-year veteran of the Canadian Forces, enlisting for a military career shortly after the landmark 1989 decision.

Personnel of the Canadian Women's Army Corps at No. 3 CWAC (Basic) Training Centre, April 6, 1944.

MARGUERITE DOWNS: MANY WAYS TO SERVE

For more than a century and half, Black Canadians have time and time again demonstrated their willingness to support their country during times of strife.

On June 4, 2009, Maj. Marguerite Downs passed away. She was the highest-ranking black female officer in the Ontario Canadian Forces Reserve. She had served in the reserves for 45 years, steadily moving up through the ranks since her enlistment in 1955 with the Royal Canadian Army Services Corps in Halifax as a driver.

Along the way, Maj. Downs became a registered nurse while raising four children alone. The demands of her military duties soundly disproved any notion that reservists were idling part-timers. She balanced them against a full-time day job and church activities that included 30 years as musical director and pianist for the Voices of Joy choir of Toronto's First Baptist Church, a church founded in 1826 by escaped slaves.

Her work within the reserves included recruitment, cadet training and counselling, evaluations and discipline. She also served four Ontario lieutenant-governors as an aide-de-camp, assisting with event organizing and protocol advice.

Throughout her military career, Maj. Downs consistently demonstrated that being a Canadian can transcend cultures and colour. Throughout her lifetime, she received many awards. Perhaps her greatest achievement was the inspiration and guidance she provided cadets and reservists to pursue continuing military careers. There is no medal for that, only respect and memories.

OUR FORCES: OVERLOOKED VALUE

The town of Oromocto, New Brunswick, gives a perfect example of the spinoff economic benefits that come from being next to a Canadian Forces base. Local folks realize it, but it slips by most who aren't there to see it.

Back in the mid-19th century, still the age of sail, Oromocto was a thriving shipbuilding centre. It wasn't long, however, before steel hulls and steam put an end to those industries. A town of a thousand souls shrunk to a few dozen, and there its population seemed destined to stay.

Then, in 1952, the Canadian military decided to build a new forces base: Gagetown, now CFB Gagetown. The new base bordered on Oromocto and suddenly, the backwater town was struck by a surge of prosperity that still resonates today.

The town's population today is approaching 8,500 (out of which 600 Oromocto civilians work on the base). Many others provide services to the base and/or its 3,000 military personnel. In New Brunswick, a province often plagued by high unemployment and few opportunities, these are significant numbers. In fact, with expanded and diversified services to accommodate the base's needs, the town has become an attractive bedroom community to civil servants and others in Fredericton, the province's capital, 20 kilometres away.

The town of Petawawa, Ontario, has similarly benefited from its location on the edge of a Canadian Forces base. Initially, Petawawa grew up around its forestry industry. Then, in 1905, the Canadian Army started acquiring land to build a new base. Close to Ottawa, the natural terrain of dense bush, rock, and the Ottawa River provided an excellent training environment.

As with Oromocto, the town of Petawawa provides services and a pool of civilian workers for the base. While the timber industry in the region has stagnated in recent decades, Petawawa continues to grow. Today, it has a population of over 15,000.

CANADIAN FORCES CURRENT STRENGTH

Land Forces: 19,500
Air Forces: 12,500
Naval Forces: 9,000
Support Services: 20,000
Reservists: 27,000

CADET CORPS
Royal Canadian Army Cadets: 21,000
Royal Canadian Air Cadets: 24,500
Royal Canadian Navy Cadets and Navy League Cadets: 15,000

PRINSENDAM, SOS

By the fall of 1980, the air crew of the Argus Mk-1, Number 10721 of 407 (Maritime Patrol) Squadron based at RCAF Station/CFB Comox knew the dependable old plane was months away from being replaced by a CP-140 Aurora. What the crew didn't know was that before it was taken off the books, the Argus would be called on to participate in perhaps the greatest peacetime air-sea rescue in history.

On the night of October 4, 1980, CFB Comox received a call for support from the U.S. Coast Guard Rescue Co-ordination Centre in Juneau, Alaska. Just over 1,000 kilometres from Comox and 224 kilometres from the nearest Alaskan coastal community, Yakutut, the Holland America cruise ship, *Prinsendam*, carrying 524 passengers and crew, was afire. By 5 a.m., the order to abandon ship had been given.

Answering the Call

The 407's Argus, together with two Buffalo search planes, and two CH-46 Labrador helicopters with search and rescue and medical teams from 442 Squadron were dispatched to the scene in the Gulf of Alaska.

The 128-metre, six-deck *Prinsendam* was three days into a 24-day cruise that had begun in Vancouver and was scheduled to travel the Inland Passage to Ketchikan, then move on to Japan, Shanghai, Hong Kong and Singapore, before returning to Vancouver. Now, just hours after leaving Ketchikan, the ship threatened to become a fiery grave or a frigid watery tomb.

Along with the Canadian military contingent, five U.S. Coast Guard and U.S. Air Force helicopters and cutters were en route. Fortunately, the 300-metre super tanker *Williamsburg* was within 165 kilometres of the stricken ship.

By the time rescuers began arriving, the weather had thickened, and the seas become heavier. Many of the lifeboats, designed for 60 people, were crowded with as many as 90. In all, six lifeboats and four inflatable rafts were launched from the *Prinsendam*.

One Canadian helicopter lost its navigational aids as it approached, then experienced a generator fire — and this in thick fog. A USAF Hercules eventually shepherded it to Yakutut, where its search and rescue personnel boarded a U.S. helicopter, and its medical team was transferred to the *Williamsburg*, which had helipads.

Race Against Time

Time constraints were in the red zone; the tail end of a typhoon was expected to sweep the area within a few hours. Already six-metre seas and rising winds were threatening to capsize the lifeboats. The only option for rescuers was to hoist the survivors into the hovering helicopters and transport them to the *Williamsburg* and other ships.

Many of the passengers were elderly, others were accompanied by small children; they had already been up much of the night. The main lounge of the cruise ship was so smoky, passengers had been evacuated to the open promenade deck.

A smaller bar, the Prins Club, was opened to provide free drinks; the gift shop handed out free sweaters to many passengers who were clad only in nightwear; and shipboard entertainers strove to maintain passenger morale, reminiscent of the orchestra on the *Titanic*. By then, the engines and electricity were shut down, and an ominous darkness had settled over the ship and sea. Deep in the ship's engine room, the fire continued to rage. By daylight everyone was in lifeboats but still stranded.

The helicopters were limited in the number of survivors they could carry in one trip, yet safety could not be sacrificed to haste. The crew of the Canadian helicopter dropped an SAR specialist into a targeted lifeboat to organize survivors and ensure those in most distress were airlifted first. Compared to the American crews, which relied on survivors to organize themselves, the Canadian efficiency was remarkable.

Canadian Efficiency

Overall, Canadians lifted off 31 survivors, then were assigned to locate a missing lifeboat. They found it and rescued nine more passengers. Desperately low on fuel, the helicopter hovered over the lifeboat until a U.S. Coast Guard cutter arrived to take off the remaining survivors. The Canadians cut it so close to the wire that an engine flamed out as it landed at Yakutut. The nine survivors were unaware of how close their rescue had come to being its own disaster.

Throughout, the reliable Argus from Comox circled the scene and illuminated it for

Lick Them Over There! : war propaganda campaign.

rescuers with a 70-million-candlepower searchlight mounted on its starboard wing. In 1982, Argus No. 10721 succumbed to the cutting torch in a scrapyard, as unheralded as the crews from Comox who flew into the stormy Gulf of Alaska that night.

In total, 524 people were rescued from the *Prinsendam*. There were no fatalities. The ship burned itself out and sank on October 11 in 2,640 metres of water.

THE RIGHT TO KNOW

U.S. General Westmoreland blamed unrestricted media access for the widespread public resistance to the Vietnam War.

The premature entry of Canadian Forces into the Somalia conflict in 1992-93 was attributed to sensationalistic media coverage that inflamed public opinion.

Yet media coverage from the war zones of World War II was considered to be an enormous morale booster in the Allies' home countries, notably Canada. Media coverage of the Afghanistan conflict and repatriation of Canadian casualties has also resulted in a resurgence of home support and respect for the Canadian Forces.

The potential danger to correspondents reporting from conflict zones is enormous.

Nineteen journalists have been killed in Afghanistan in eight years. In conflict zones and areas of violent political or sectarian unrest, detainments, kidnappings, executions, physical beatings and threats are often genuine risks.

Embedding journalists in military units may reduce risks, but danger still dogs many stories. Clear evidence of that is found in the Canadian Forces media embedding program guidelines. Listed among "don't leave without them" items are:

Flak vest
Helmet
Ballistic eyewear
Fire-retardant gloves
Long sleeved shirt made of natural fibre that does not burn at low temperatures

In Calgary, the Canadian Defence and Foreign Affairs Institute offers a short course called the Canadian military journalism course. It isn't about writing so much as it is about survival.

The American military also provides a training program for journalists who may be embedded. Several private security firms also give field training in addition to class-room instruction. Some news agencies, such as Reuters, routinely use these programs.

No Guarantees

None of this guarantees the safety of journalists despite the best efforts of the military to protect them. During the Second World War, famous American war correspondent Ernie Pyle was killed by a Japanese sniper. More recently in Afghanistan, CanWest journalist Michelle Lang died along with four soldiers when an IED destroyed their armoured vehicle.

Reporters Without Borders recently advised that the Taliban have stepped up the targeting of journalists. Overall, 16 journalists have died worldwide at the hands of radical Islamist groups. The majority of the dead were not embedded.

Although some journalists may argue that embedded reportage results in "con-trolled" news, embedding and censorship have been commonplace at least since the Crimean War in the 19th century.

As for "control," there are often operational reasons related to secrecy and security that make censorship essential. For example, there are sections of the Kandahar base that are off limits to Canadian journalists. Some newsworthy infor-mation is embargoed, casualty reports included.

Reporting on the actions of Canada's Special Forces is forbidden, restricted solely to that officially released by the Canadian Forces itself. Graphic description or filming of troops in action is forbidden, particularly that which describes the carnage and nature of casualties.

Canada's military is constantly involved in a precarious balancing act, attempt-ing to ensure the safety of servicemen and women, provide security to journalists, enable as much access to information as is reasonably and responsibly possible and fulfilling their mission.

That the Canadian public has become hungrier for news out of Afghanistan has increased pressure on the military to provide it. If there seems to be resistance, some of it may be justified.

GETTING THE STORY

All of Canada was engaged during World War II. The Axis powers were bent on world domination which naturally constituted a genuine threat to North America.

At home, Canada was gripped by WW II, and recruitment for the military services was vigorous. The war industry had quickly pulled the country out of the Depression, but rationing of gasoline and other commodities put the weight of the war on everyone's shoulders. Sensitive to Canadians' demand for war news, Canada's journalists and the military obliged.

Canadian military services in WW II accredited 25 war correspondents. Many became household names: Matthew Halton, Peter Stursberg, Ross Munro, Charles Lynch, Margaret Armstrong, Pierre Dupuy and Don Fairbairn, to name a few. When people weren't scouring their newspapers, they were grouped attentively around their radios, tuned to the CBC.

One correspondent, Bob Bowman, was at Dieppe; others shifted from front to front — North Africa, Sicily, Italy, France, Holland, and then into Germany. El Alamein, Ortona, the Liri Valley, Juno Beach, the Scheldt and Falaise Gap, Canadian journalists were there. They were also hunkered down in London's bomb shelters during the Battle of Britain, flew on Allied bombing runs over Europe and marched, crawled and dove for cover with the infantrymen.

CBC Radio pioneered a mobile recording studio that could be shipped from front to front. For the first time, the sounds of battle reverberated in Canadian living rooms. Shortly after the liberation of Rome, CBC recorded a message to Canadians from the Pope, a first in electronic journalism.

When Hollywood finally went to war and began churning out war movies, the studios relied on the CBC recordings of actual artillery barrages to provide some realism. Many of the recordings were made by engineers positioned between the artillery and the front lines.

The Canadian military provided access to its correspondents and facilitated movement of their equipment and delivery of their dispatches and recordings, even from the Normandy beaches. Yet it was up to the journalists to find their own stories and, in the thick of that, the military provided no specific security.

Enter Korea

Reporting on the Canadian efforts in the Korean War and a multitude of peace-keeping efforts has brought another generation of journalists to the fore of conflict reporting.

Peter Worthington and Matthew Fisher are examples of this generation. Worthington continues to write authoritatively on Canadian military matters, and Fisher frequently pops up in conflict zones throughout the world in search of stories. In Afghanistan, he is considered an "old hand."

Newsgathering today is not the same as it was during World War II. News cycles, satellite communication and same-day reporting have added urgency to the equation. The amorphous nature of many conflicts, especially those which fully involve civilians, such as in Afghanistan, require closer military involvement.

If the universality and speed of communications that characterized the Vietnam War has taught one important military lesson, it is that enemies also watch television. And now, of course, they also monitor the Internet, YouTube, Facebook and Twitter.

INK FROM OUTSIDE THE WIRE

Scott Taylor and David Pugliese are two veteran military journalists who have been reporting from the world's hot spots for more than two decades.

Scott Taylor brings a "boots-on-the-ground" soldier's perspective—— and survival instinct — to his military journalism, which began in 1988 when he became the publisher and editor of *Esprit de Corps*, the most candid, contentious, and perhaps, informed defence periodical in Canada.

Over the years, he has reported from the Persian Gulf, Western Sahara, the Balkans, Yugoslavia, Azerbaijan, and Afghanistan. In 2004, he was briefly held hostage by Islamic mujahedeen in northern Iraq. About 18 months earlier, he was strongly advised to leave Iraq because of suspicions he was an Israeli spy. In a further twist to his Iraq experiences, he later spent some time advising U.S. military authorities on Iraqi tribal customs.

Taylor is one of the very few Canadian journalists who (for the most part)

War correspondent Benoit Lafleur of the Canadian Broadcasting Corporation near San Vito Chietino, Italy on April 8th, 1944.

pursue their stories unembedded. In fact, his 2009 memoir is titled *Unembedded: Two Decades of Maverick War Reporting*.

He has not only been "in the thick of it" with Canadian and other UN and NATO soldiers in the field; he has taken his early background as a professional soldier, melded it with probing investigative journalism and produced work that in some respects has compelled Canada's military brass to take a hard look at itself and the way it operates.

Unlike Taylor, David Pugliese is not a former soldier, though he is equally an authority on Canadian military matters and defence policy. Since he began reporting on the military in the mid-1980s, Pugliese has won three National Newspaper Awards for his work.

Pugliese has a particular interest in military training and is a familiar face on many Canadian bases. He has written authoritative books about the training and operations of JTF2, Canada's elite, secretive, special operations unit, while most Canadian journalists would have a difficult time getting any access whatsoever to them, let alone obtaining operations information.

Like Taylor, Pugliese is a much-travelled journalist. His passport has stamps from such conflict zones as the Balkans, Sudan, Afghanistan, Haiti, the Philippines, and Burma. He has also reported from the volatile Gaza Strip and northern Pakistan.

FRONT-LINE AIRPORTS

During the past 60 years, the Canadian Forces have become familiar with many airports around the world, and not only because its members travel a lot.

Consider these locations:

The name Kandahar is well-known now to Canadians who read newspapers, surf the Internet or watch the evening news. This sprawling airbase is Action Central for Canadian Forces in Afghanistan. Troop rotations come through Kandahar, as do all supplies and equipment. The helicopter crews servicing Canadian-manned remote outposts and major offensives into Taliban country also operate from here.

While Kandahar is strictly a military airbase, the Canadian Forces experience includes many airports – in the Congo, for example, where an airport may be nothing but a single strip hurriedly cleared by bulldozers to enable relief supply planes to land. Others among the five also serve as international airports.

Templehof Airport

One international airport is Berlin's Templehof Airport. Here, between June 1948 and May 1949, more than 200,000 relief flights supplied more than 13 million tons of food, medical supplies, and other goods during the Berlin Airlift, which broke the Soviet blockade of the city. The fourth-largest air force in the world by the end of World War II, the RCAF played a vital role in this U.S.-led achievement, considered a major victory for the West in the Cold War.

Nicosia International Airport

The Nicosia International Airport in Cyprus became a focal point in 1974 for another significant Canadian Forces achievement. Here, at the height of the Turkish invasion of the island, Canadian Brig.-Gen. Clay Beattie ordered his small contingent of the Canadian Airborne Regiment, the lead force of the Cyprus UN peacekeeping mission, to hold the airport.

The Canadians had already taken casualties from both Turkish and Greek fire. They had no illusions that peacekeeping remained their main mission. It had been replaced by peacemaking, and even that was a fragile business.

As for the airport, it was the key to control of the island, and if either the Turkish or the Greek army forced the issue, untold civilian casualties were a likely result. Moreover, the UN force would be cut off, and evacuation of non-belligerents would be impossible.

The Airborne had only light arms, all that the UN rules of engagement permitted. Arranged around the airport were Turkish tanks, artillery, and other heavy weapons. Turkish officers threatened to attack. Already the airport had been subject to both Turkish and Greek mortar fire as well as air strikes by the Turkish Air Force. The Canadians refused to back down, making it clear they would defend the airport.

The tense standoff ended when the Turks and Greeks agreed to a tentative truce. The Canadian determination to defend the airport had not been a bluff. Although they knew they would certainly be overwhelmed if the Turkish army assaulted the airport, the consequences of surrender outweighed that potential outcome.

The Airborne had in effect bought the UN time to work out the truce. For the first time, notice was served that the UN would do more than idly watch belligerent nations run roughshod over each other and anyone else who got in their way.

Sarajevo International Airport

In 1992, journalists turned the eyes of the world to Sarajevo, a city under siege. Mortar fire hammered the city daily. The civilian population's only lifeline was relief supplies flown in to the Sarajevo airport.

Squarely caught in the middle of a shooting war of attrition was a UN peacekeeping force commanded by Canadian Maj.-Gen. Lewis MacKenzie. Based at the airport, he was pressured to negotiate intermittent ceasefires enabling the supply planes to land.

Much of MacKenzie's success hinged on the bargaining leverage he obtained by winning over international journalists who found working stories from the airport less risky than in the city itself. Disfavour in the media would hurt both sides of the conflict because their war also involved a propaganda battle for public support. In effect, as they were aware, the airport was the world's press room, and MacKenzie was the lead news source.

That fact, however, didn't make the airport exempt from periodic shelling. When France's Premier Francois Mitterrand decided to drop in to see the situation for himself, MacKenzie had to buy time in order to ensure the runway could be cleared of shell fragments and other debris.

The battles in the former Yugoslavia would drag on for another four years, requiring a Canadian Forces presence throughout, but victory in the public relations battle of the Sarajevo airport definitely went to Canada and the United Nations.

Jacmel

In recent times, the small airport at Haiti's second-largest port city, Jacmel, stands out as the site of one of the Canadian Forces' finest moments. In the early days following the January 2010 earthquake in Haiti, the country's main airport at Port-au-Prince was at a virtual standstill. Its air traffic control capability had been destroyed. Almost within hours of the earthquake, the tarmac was clogged with mountains of relief supplies and planes unable to take off because only one runway was open.

More planes were stacked above the airport waiting for an opportunity to land. Non-Haitians milled about waiting for evacuation, or in the case of aid workers, waiting impatiently for instructions. Many injured Haitians had also made their way to the airport hoping to find medical assistance.

A Canadian Forces Disaster Assistance Response Team decided the best use of Canadian resources would be to establish Canadian relief operations in Jacmel, bypassing Port-au-Prince.

The first priority was to get the airport up and running, and in a very short time this was achieved, at least to the point that flights were coming in and going out around the clock while Port-au-Prince was still in chaos. Canada's DART was among the first contingents in Jacmel.

Shortly after their arrival, Canadian heavy-lift CC-117 Globemaster IIIs flew in a fully-equipped field hospital. By the time a Canadian Forces frigate and destroyer arrived at the port, Canadian Forces engineers had the facilities ready for them.

The Forces' almost seamless response to the disaster was a textbook best-practices example of how capable the Canadian military has become in such circumstances.

HOME AWAY FROM HOME COOKIN'

Recently, a Canadian Forces CH-146 Griffon helicopter en route from Edmonton to Thunder Bay made a quick stop on a ball diamond in Kenora, Ontario. A crewman crossed the street to an A & W and picked up an order of Papa Burgers — supper for the air crew.

According to another report, until the practice was banned by the base commander, helicopters from CFB Shiloh made occasional runs to a local McDonald's.

Infantrymen of The Argyll and Sutherland Highlanders of Canada cooking a meal and warming themselves around a fire in a barnyard near Veen, Germany, March 7, 1945.

Sure, one of the most popular Canadian Forces hangouts at the Kandahar Air Base in Afghanistan is a Tim Hortons but that's "official," as are the seven 'Timmies' on bases across Canada. Indeed, Canadian Forces Maritime Atlantic Command recently issued a sole-source tender call for a Tim Hortons, based on personnel preference. No substitutes need apply.

Certainly, feeding the troops is now taken seriously in the Canadian Forces, as it should be. Outside the Kandahar main base at small Canadian field bases, well-equipped kitchen trailers are brought in to prepare meals. The cooks, if they're good, are often bragged about by the units they feed.

Given Afghanistan's isolated, cramped field conditions for troops outside the wire — heat, dust, threat of attack — many of the meals coming out of the "slop shops" are masterpieces. The *Globe & Mail's* Jessica Leeder described one meal, admittedly a bit of an exception from the norm. The menu: beef tenderloin and steamed crab legs, grilled onions and peppers, baked mushrooms and scratch mushroom basil sauce, salads and cheeses, with cakes and ice cream to top it off —everything but a selection of vintage wines. It at least shows what the chefs are capable of preparing.

Menus are diverse; there are hot meals daily, often including hot breakfast options, and entrees one would find on the menus of many full-service restaurants or in Mom's kitchen.

Eating Out

A lot of attention has also been paid to rations for Canadian troops on the move. These are called individual meal packs, or IMPs. The entrees are designed to be eaten hot or cold. IMPs usually offer six options each for breakfast, lunch, and supper. More likely, choice depends on what's available in the unit stores. From that list, below is a random selection. Option one for breakfast, option two for lunch, and option three for supper would be:

Breakfast

Ham steak with mustard sauce

Sliced pears with syrup

Crunchy cereal

Orange beverage crystals

Bread

Honey x 2

Coffee x 2

Sugar x 2

Whitener x2

Hot chocolate mix (hazel nut cream flavour)

Ketchup

Green striped mint candy

Chewing gum

Lunch

Pork with herbs and wine sauce

Sliced apples with syrup

Orange beverage crystals

Bread

Peanut butter × 2

Instant tomato basil-flavoured rice

Mustard

Coffee × 2

Sugar × 2

Whitener × 2

Dairy Milk chocolate bar

Green striped mint candy

Supper

Chicken breast cacciatore

Sliced pears with syrup

Orange beverage crystals

Cream of celery soup

Bread

Honey × 2

Instant tomato basil flavoured rice

Pepper sauce

Coffee

Regular Tea

Sugar × 2

Whitener × 2

Mocha pudding

Strawberry flavoured cream candy

Each IMP comes with salt and pepper, paper towel and moist towelette, matches, a toothpick and a plastic spoon. With no knife or fork on the list, that spoon may say something about what's in those meal baggies, but it looks great on paper.

PUTTING ON THE FEED BAG

During the Boer War and World War I, Canadian forces generally followed the British lead in provisioning troops, probably because they were under British command. Recruits were always checked for strong healthy teeth. During the Boer War, Canadian troop rations usually consisted of tea, tinned bully beef (corned beef as we know it), and hardtack, emphasis on the "hard" – think dog biscuits. Hot meals were rare. Troops routinely dipped into the horse feed to fill their stomachs.

The situation improved during World War I, at least on paper. In 1914, the ideal daily British ration included:

1-1/4 lb. fresh or frozen meat, or 1 lb. preserved or salt meat (bully beef)

1-1/4 lb. bread, or 1 lb. biscuit or flour

4 oz. bacon

3 oz. cheese

5/8 oz. tea

4 oz. jam

3 oz. sugar

½ oz. salt

1/36 oz. pepper

1/20 oz. mustard

8 oz. fresh or 2 oz. dried vegetables

1/10 gill lime juice (if fresh vegetables not issued)

½ gill rum (at discretion of commanding officer)

2 oz. tobacco per week (at discretion of commanding officer)

As the war dragged on, rations for soldiers in the trenches were considerably reduced, to the point where significant military advances were delayed or halted by lack of food. Transportation was a serious problem on the Western Front. Because of enemy artillery fire, field kitchens were often miles from the front. Sometimes, it took eight days to get bread to the troops in the trenches.

Perhaps to demoralize the Germans, who were suffering worse food shortages, the British government announced that two hot meals were provided daily to its troops. The backlash was 200,000 "very public" letters from soldiers begging to differ. Audacity turned to embarrassment.

Canadian Resourcefulness

Along the Western Front, Canadians were often in the same locale for months. Sometimes they could forage or barter to supplement their rations. No one got a medal for these quasi-clandestine food patrols, but a couple of eggs or a tough old laying hen was mouth-watering reward enough.

In the mid-1920s, Canadian military minds decided to go it alone on food supply. By World War II, Canadians had developed their own system for feeding troops. Most of it was accepted by troops, but emergency rations were eloquently scorned by soldiers, who loathed Necco Wafers, a type of candy that did not melt, and chocolate nut cake, or whatever it was.

Wars have been lost because troops weren't properly fed. Providing X number of calories per day may work for nutritionists and war planners. But for a soldier in the field, palatable food should be more than just a treat. If a Papa Burger or Quarter Pounder is what it takes, planners should work it out.

Master Corporal Angela Abbey, Canadian Forces Combat Camera, DND IS2009-3029

Piper, Sergeant James Douglas, observes a moment of silence during a remembrance service held at the Vimy Ridge National Memorial Site of Canada, in France.

AFTERWORD

2011 is the year Canada will be reducing its troops assignation in Afghanistan to 950 trainer/instructors. This may not bode well for the future state of the Canadian Forces.

Canada has for generations expected a great deal from its military but has only reluctantly provided them the means; the tools, training, and human resources, to satisfy these expectations.

Clearly, during the 65 years that have passed since the end of World War II, Canadians should have learned that peace has a price. In our cash nexus culture, only hard currency is acceptable, rhetoric cannot be taken to the bank. The Canadian Forces have learned this, often at the cost of members' lives.

It has been said that no Canadian politician ever lost a vote by cutting the country's military budget, and today all signs point to further budget cuts. This at a time when the military has finally begun to recover and modernize after crippling cuts in the 80s and 90s, and to recover from crippling apathy in terms of public military acceptance and support.

Overzealous cutbacks after World War I left our military scrambling at the outset of World War II. Post-WW II cutbacks left our military scrambling again as it went into the Korean conflict, and as it tried to meet the country's NATO and NORAD commitments during the Cold War. The collapse of the USSR and the end of the Cold War were again seen as good reason to slash the military budget, while Canada's U.N. and NATO obligations increased in other world conflict zones.

Historically, Canada's state of military readiness has been punctuated by reliance on torpedoes without explosives (WW I), wooden naval guns (WW II), borrowed uniforms (Gulf War), leased and borrowed helicopters (Afghanistan).

The Canadian Forces deserve better. They need it and they have earned it.

FURTHER READING

Andrews, Allen. Brave Soldiers, Proud Regiments: Canada's Military Heritage. Toronto: Ronsdale Press, 1997.

Beattie, Clay. The Bulletproof Flag: Canadian Peacekeeping Forces and the War in Cyprus. Maxville, Ontario: Optimum Publishing, 2007.

Borda, Jenifer. War and Peacekeeping. Toronto: Rubicon Education Inc., 2002.

Dallaire, Romeo. Shake Hands with the Devil. Toronto: Random House, 2003.

Dancocks, Daniel G. The D-Day Dodgers: The Canadians in Italy, 1943-1945. Edmonton: Hurtig Publishers, 1983.

Granatstein, J.L. & David Bercuson. War and Peacekeeping: From South Africa to the Gulf – Canada's Limited Wars. Toronto: Key Porter Books, 1991.

Horn, Col. Bernd, ed. The Canadian Way of War: Serving the National Interest. Toronto: Dundurn Press, 2006.

MacKenzie, Lewis. Peacekeeper: The Road to Sarajevo. Vancouver: Douglas and McIntyre, 2008.

MacPherson, Ken & John Burgess. The Ships of Canada's Naval Forces, 1910-1985. Toronto: Collins, 1985.

Meyers, Edward C. Thunder in the Morning Calm: The RCN in Korea, 1950-1955. St. Catherines: Vanwell Publishing, 1992.

Milner, Marc. Canada's Navy: The First Century. Toronto: University of Toronto Press, 1999.

Nicholson, G.W.L. Canada's Nursing Sisters. Toronto: A.M. Hakkert Ltd., 1975.

Redman Stanley R. Open Gangway: The (Real) Story of the Halifax Navy Riot. Hontsport, N.S.: Lancelot Press, 1990.

Swettenham, J. Canada's Atlantic War. Toronto: Samuel-Stevens, 1979.